AF574611

FIELD GUIDE
TO BRITISH
WILD
FLOWERS

FIELD GUIDE TO BRITISH
WILD FLOWERS

MAURICE BURTON

OCTOPUS
BOOKS

Acknowledgements
The author acknowledges the help obtained from *English Names of Wild Flowers:* a recommended list of the Botanical Society of the British Isles. All common and scientific names are consistent with those that appear in this book.

Colour Plates
Richard Bonson and Anthony Morris

Illustrations
Pages 8-26 Gill Tomblin

Photographs
Jane Burton

First published in 1982

This edition published in 1984 by Octopus Books Limited 59 Grosvenor Street, London W1

ISBN 0 7064 2091 8

Printed in Hong Kong

Contents

Introduction

Since well over a thousand different wild flowers can be found growing in Britain it has been necessary to be rigidly selective in choosing which to include in this book. However, the 160 species covered do give a taste of the botanical treasures that our countryside has to offer. In making this selection the numerous grasses, sedges and most of the rushes have been excluded. So too have all trees and shrubs. Ferns, horsetails, liverworts and mosses have also been omitted since they are not flowering plants.

Even so, having narrowed the field in this way, the problem of what to include still remained. The aim of the book is to delight the eye, so the temptation was strong to concentrate on the more showy and colourful flowers, but to have done so would have meant having to omit many interesting plants, as well as presenting an unbalanced survey of our native flora. Introduced species, of which several are widespread and well established, have been excluded.

After this further pruning we were still left with a bewildering array of species, each clamouring to be given pride of place. One consideration, however, seemed of paramount importance: that some idea should be given of plant classification. This satisfies not only our sense of tidiness but also our curiosity. A botanist experiences contentment and pride in being able to 'put a name to' any plant; and non-botanists enjoy these feelings even if they can do no more than name the family to which the plant belongs.

There are some 57 different families of wild flowers even within the field to which our survey has been narrowed. Some of these are represented by no more than a handful of species, but others, such as the Daisy and Mint families are made up of dozens or scores. Therefore, to preserve a balance, these should be represented by a greater number of species than a family having only two or three. The next difficulty lay in choosing from these large families the few species that could be included.

Naturally, to some extent, our final choice was influenced by personal familiarity with, or preference for, a particular species, but there were, however, more logical factors at work. Since this book is intended for the general reader rather than the professional botanist, it was obviously best to single out those flowers most likely to be found in the garden or on a country ramble. Nevertheless, wild flowers have their own preferences in the matter of habitat and we have assumed that the reader will not be restricting his activities to lowland fields, hedges and gardens.

The more neglected a garden, the richer it will be in wild flowers. The dedicated gardener calls them weeds; yet these weeds are often extremely attractive and can be of great interest to anyone who knows about their structure, way of life and botanical history. Weeds are not always unwelcome, so think twice before removing one from your border to make way for a cultivated flower.

Plant distribution

Two million years ago, what is now the British Isles was invaded by a vast ice sheet that reached south as far as the Thames and then retreated northwards again. This happened four times, constituting what is known as the Ice Age. The last retreat of the ice sheet began 14,000 years ago. The grinding of the glaciers composing it, as well as the constant low temperatures, killed off the vegetation and reduced the land to waste except for the few alpine plants capable of existing under such conditions. Even when the temperature had risen the land was subject to rushing waters from the melting of ice. Like a building site, the ground lacked adequate humus and only a few hardy weeds, notably Chickweed, began to recolonize it.

In time, but extremely slowly, these were joined by other plants spreading northwards from the continent of Europe. However, this was hampered by the submergence, about 10,000 years ago, of the landbridge joining Britain to northern France.

What happens to seeds when they arrive at their final destination is decided by the kind of soil they land on and their own preferences, as well as the temperatures and humidity of the air and soil. A striking example of the effect of humidity concerns a spectacular growth of Marsh-marigolds. This was on what had been, until early in the 1950s, a piece of dry pastureland adjacent to a stream. A main sewer had to be taken across it and in the process an old drain became damaged with the result that the previously dry meadow reverted to marsh. Within a few years the marsh became covered in May with the golden blossoms of the Marsh-marigold.

It is possible to tell where outcrops of limestone appear on a heather moor by the colour of the grass, and of course the wild flowers.

Cross-leaved Heath and Tormentil are acid-lovers, while Field Scabious and Common Bird's-foot-trefoil prefer lime.

Seeds from plants that flourish best on a chalky soil will stand little chance if they drop on to an acid one. Heather moors are the best example of an acid soil habitat. Sometimes on such moors there will be outcrops of limestone, not obvious to the eye except that the vegetation is different. Anyone with good colour vision can tell where the acid soil ends and the limy one begins, by the colour of the grass. When the flowers growing on the respective soils are noted it becomes clear that there are two distinct floras: acid-lovers and lime-lovers.

So we could go on. A plant that prefers dry land has little chance in a bog. Some plants grow best on disturbed soils; others need ground that is not ploughed up or dug over. Flowers growing on sand dunes are unlike those that are found on moist clay.

These are only a few factors that determine the pattern of wild flowers in any stretch of countryside. Another is the influence of trees. There is evidence that trees and shrubs did not begin to return to Britain until 9,000 years ago. In due course most of the country became forested. Neolithic farmers reached Britain 3,000 years ago and began the process of felling trees which has continued ever since. Yet left to itself Britain would in the end again become how the Neolithic farmers found it: a land of forests interspersed with bogs and lakes.

The bed of Marsh-marigolds already mentioned became invaded by sedges, rushes and coarse grasses, and by a massive growth of Willow Herb, each in succession. Now willow saplings have begun to appear. It can be predicted that alders and then other trees will follow and in due course this piece of land will be a small oak forest. The succession will then have reached its climax and the mere presence of the trees and their canopy, which shuts out the light during the growing season of the year, will have revolutionized the flowers growing on the ground beneath.

Flower structure

The shapes and forms of flowers vary enormously, yet all are modifications of a simple basic plan. This idealized plan is very close to what can be seen in a Buttercup. We can start with the flower stalk which ends in a fleshy head known as the receptacle. On this is seated a series of floral organs. The first of these is the calyx, made up of a circle of green sepals. Inside this are the petals which collectively form the corolla. Sometimes all the sepals are joined to form a tube, and sometimes the petals are also. Usually, in such cases, the number of sepals and the number of petals are indicated by the lobes on the free margins.

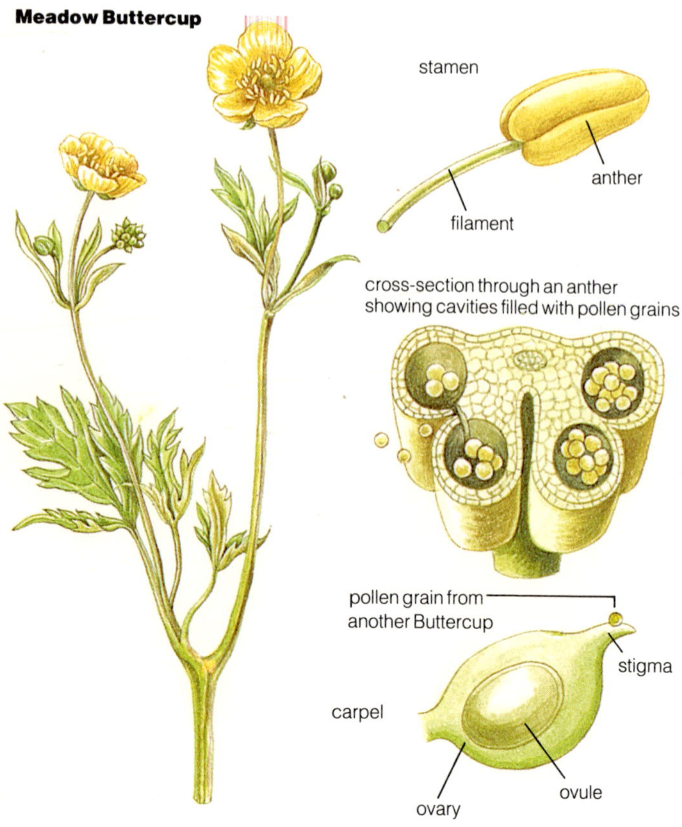

Within the corolla are two more series, both very different from the first two. These are the stamens and the pistil, the reproductive organs of the flower. A stamen consists of a stalk, called its filament, which carries the anther, or pollen sac. The pollen is a sort of powder made up of numerous small grains, the pollen grains or male reproductive cells. The pistil is composed of an enlarged base, the ovary, from which rises a slender rod, the style, at the top of which is a small sticky cushion, known as the stigma.

Pollen grains falling on the stigma each sends a long slender tube to the ovary which contains the ovules or egg-cells.

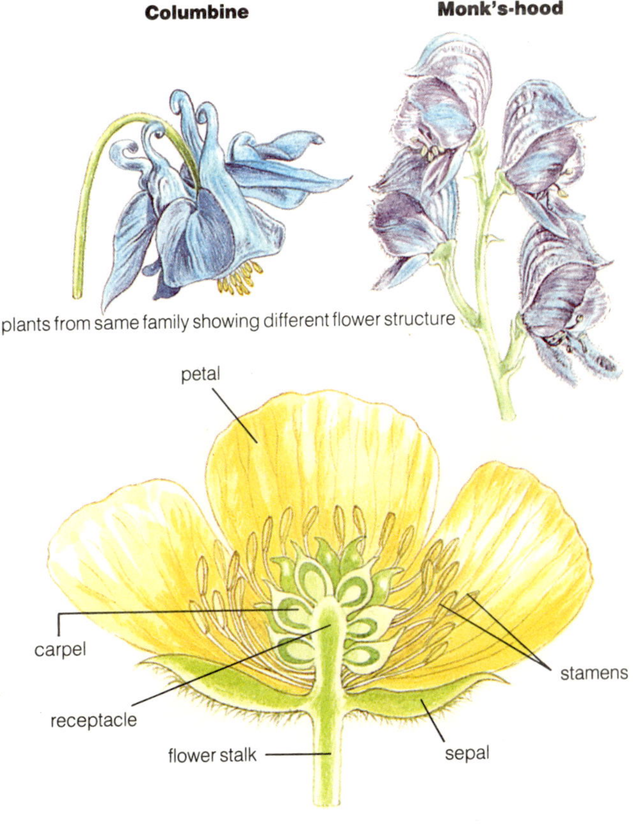

plants from same family showing different flower structure

cross-section of Buttercup flower

Types of flower

Flowering plants are divided into two main groups: the monocotyledons and the dicotyledons. A cotyledon is a seed-leaf, the first leaf to spring from the germinating seed. Monocotyledons usually grow from bulbs or corms. Their seeds throw out only one seed-leaf. The leaves are blade-like but, more importantly, the parts of the flower are in threes, or multiples of three, as is well seen in the Iris.

The seeds of the dicotyledons have two seed-leaves, their leaves are all kinds of shapes and the parts of the flower are most commonly in fives, or multiples of five. The Buttercup is a good example. However, the parts may be in fours, as in the Cabbage family, giving a cross-shape, hence the scientific name *Cruciferae*. Two more notable families with unusual flowers are the Pea family *(Leguminosae)* and the Mint family *(Labiatae)*, each with numerous species.

The flowers of the Pea family are the most distinctive in the British flora. One of the five petals forms a hood over the other four. Beneath this are two lateral petals that enclose the final two which are fused to form a keel or boat-shape.

The flowers of the *Labiatae* look like snapdragons. Their flowers are tubular and end in two lobe-like lips.

Another very large family is the *Compositae*, the Daisy family, with composite flowers, each flowerhead made up of a central disc of small florets around which radiate petal-like florets.

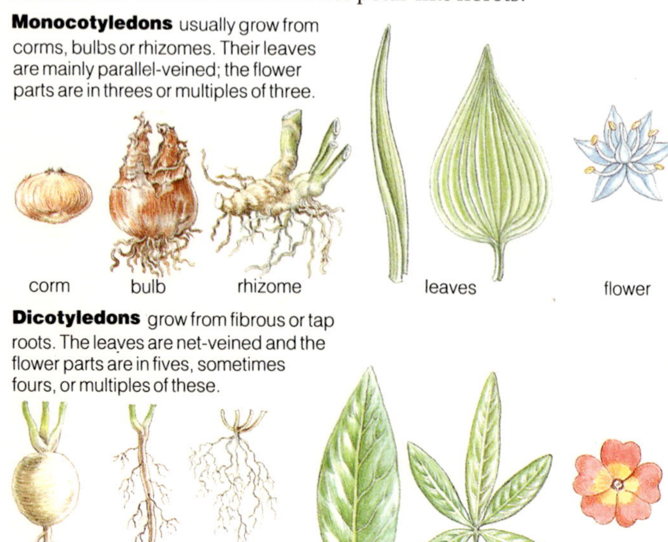

Yellow Iris
a monocotyledon
Marsh-marigold
four dicotyledons
Spotted
Deadnettle
Daisy
Common Vetch

Seed dispersal

If a plant were to drop its seeds straight on to the ground below, the seedlings from them would have to compete for light, air and nourishment from the soil, not only with each other but also with the parent plant. So every plant has to have some means of dispersing its seeds and many have extremely ingenious mechanisms for doing this. The seeds are scattered distances varying from a few centimetres to several metres, or considerably more when they are carried by the wind or on the feet or feathers of migrating birds. As a result, the distribution of plants varies greatly, a few species, for example Shepherd's-purse, growing almost all over the world.

Dandelion
Parachute formed by pappus enables seed to be carried away on the wind
Old Man's Beard
The feather down ensures the seed floats away from the parent plant

Spear Thistle
The wind catching the feathery hairs on the seeds carries them for miles
Willowherb
Each seed bears a tuft of silky hairs and often floats great distances

Elm
The winged seed spirals down to the ground, or is caught by the wind
Common Poppy
Every breeze or disturbance by animals scatters the ripe seeds

Violet
On drying, the capsule springs open ejecting the seeds
Crane's-bill
The capsule on drying flies open scattering the seeds

Seeds that are dispersed by the wind are usually small and therefore light, often no larger than grains of dust, or else they have some form of feathery pappus, or parachute, which enables the wind to lift them and carry them long distances. A few seeds have some form of wing and once airborne they plane down to land a fair distance from the parent plant. Others have little hooks and use animals, birds and even humans as a means of transport by attaching themselves to fur, feathers or clothing. In the case of soft fruits, such as strawberries, raspberries and blackcurrants, which are eaten by animals or birds the seeds are voided elsewhere.

Dog Rose
Birds eat the fleshy pulp of the hips, allowing the seeds to fall to the earth

Strawberry
Pulp fruits are eaten by animals or birds and the seeds pass out with the excrement

Hazel
Hazel nuts are carried away by animals such as squirrels and long-tailed field mice. Some are stored and those not eaten germinate

Acorn
Jays and squirrels bury acorns over a wide area for future use. Those not found grow into seedling oaks.

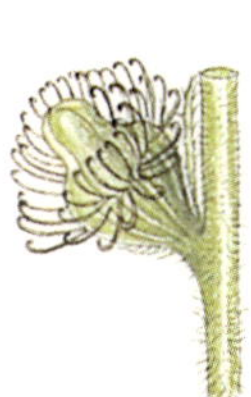

Agrimony
The seed heads of this plant are caught by their hooks on animal coats

Wood Avens
The hooked seeds attach themselves to clothing or the fur of animals and are thus dispersed

Burdock
A typical burr with its many hooks which cling to the wool of sheep and the coats of other animals

Teasel
A toothed bract, one of the many making up the egg-shaped head of the Teasel. Each contains a tiny seed. Dispersed by animals.

Photographing wild flowers

Wild flowers are often colourful and showy, and make attractive subjects for photography. There are particular problems in picturing them successfully but, as in any branch of photography, a seeing eye and a love of the subject is more important than expensive equipment.

Almost any camera can be used to take satisfactory and rewarding pictures of flowers; and most general-purpose lenses give good results when one is photographing whole plants and their habitats. Many wild flowers, however, are quite small subjects and for close-ups extension tubes are needed. More convenient for close-up work are the specially computed macro-lenses which give excellent definition. Lenses of short focal length are useful for working in confined conditions and for the landscape type of habitat shot. Longer lenses allow the photographer to work at a more comfortable distance from the subject, but the longer the focal length, the greater the risk of hand-shake.

The state of the weather is of course of great importance in flower

Extension tubes are necessary for photographing details of the structure of flowers. Always use a tripod when taking photographs close up; otherwise wind- and camera-shake can spoil the results.

A macro-lens is useful for taking portraits of flowers of buttercup size. Most standard lenses with macro-focusing will reproduce a flower at half lifesize on the film.

photography. Few people would attempt to take pictures in a downpour yet a brilliant sunny day might not be ideal either. Bright sunshine casts heavy shadows which can produce too confused a pattern, with burnt-out colourless areas in the sunlit parts and no detail in the dense shadows. Hazy sunshine or diffused lighting can give the best results, and on a sunny day it is often better to photograph a plant in your own shadow, rather than in direct sunlight. The blue colour the sky casts into shade on a clear day can be simply overcome by the use of a pink skylight filter. For close-up studies of small plants with intricate flowers and leaves, and for white flowers whose petals easily become burnt out, the diffused light of overcast days is best. However, for wide-angle shots of masses of brightly coloured flowers, or for portraits that need to show a large area of the habitat, then sunshine provides excellent lighting, especially if it is coming from one side. Bright sunlight directly behind the camera is rarely satisfactory. However, sunlight behind the subject can be an extremely rewarding form of lighting. An efficient lens hood and

Different lighting conditions bring out the different qualities of flowers. Side lighting shows texture and detail, but bright sunshine has too harsh and contrasting an effect, as it casts dense shadows.

Diffused light avoids contrasting highlights and shadows by providing graduated tones and colours. Hazy sun or light cloud give the best conditions for photographing bright – or light-petalled flowers.

reasonable care will avoid the sun hitting the lens direct and causing flare, which is the main danger from this lighting. If this problem is overcome, the back light shining through translucent veined petals and catching every little hair on leaf and stem transforms the most mundane flower subject into a truly exciting picture.

Often the main problem with photographing flowers in the wild is not so much light as movement. Plants are rarely still, the slightest breeze causing them to sway or tremble. In windy weather it is useless even to attempt photography, but on calmer days there are at least occasional lulls and one just has to wait for these pauses. Subject movement like camera-shake destroys the sharpness of image even at quite short exposures, but the camera is easier to steady than the flower: the use of a good firm tripod and a cable release will eliminate hand-shake.

One way to solve the problem of movement either of camera or subject or both is to use flash. A small transistorized unit can be mounted on a ball-and-socket head on a short arm screwed on to the

Back lighting, with strong light shining through translucent petals or bouncing off brightly reflecting ones, can produce exciting visual effects. Always take a light reading from close to the flower.

Flash tends to produce heavy shadow but is excellent for bringing out texture and colour. The shadow can readily be filled in with light bounced from a white card.

camera and can be angled on to the subject from the side. A piece of light card on the opposite side of the flower will reflect light back and fill in the shadows. Often flash can be mixed with diffused daylight to good effect: the flash adds sparkle and the daylight softens the dense shadows. Using flash means you can set a faster speed.

Whatever lighting method is used, care should be taken not only with the centre of interest, the flower itself, but with its surroundings and background. It is often necessary to tidy away dead stems and other obtrusive material, but extensive alteration to the habitat is dishonest and in no circumstances should the plant be dug up and moved to a 'better' position. Choice of camera angle often helps to eliminate distracting areas in the foreground and background. Sometimes a black or coloured card can be positioned behind the plant if a plain background is desirable; or if a low angle is appropriate the sky can be used as a very effective natural plain background. When using a long lens, sharp focus on the plant helps isolate it from the background and also conveys a sense of spaciousness.

A distracting background can be eliminated by propping a sheet of card behind the plant. Light flowers generally look best against a dark background, which also shows their shape clearly.

Another way to reduce distraction in the background is to use differential focus. With a long focus lens and large aperture, focus on the flower so that the background becomes a blur.

Illustrating wild flowers

Anyone with an interest in flowers will profit from learning how to draw and paint them accurately. Students of botany must produce illustrations, even if they lack artistic talent, as it is the only way to get to know how a plant is constructed, what its various parts are, and how it lives.

When drawing or painting a plant, begin by making notes of the species, the location, the time of the year, and the habitat. It is preferable to illustrate the whole plant, together with an indication of its habitat but, if this is not possible, concentrate on one stem and show the leaves, buds or flowers. You will want to include as much detail as possible so you must examine the flower carefully, preferably under a magnifying glass. Do enlarged rough details of its various parts – the stamens, ovary, petals, sepals, etc. and make notes of the overall size of the plant and its constituents.

Leaves often vary from the base to the stem and so where they differ draw a basal leaf and a stem leaf, showing how they are attached to the main stem, i.e. whether they have a sheathed base, a stem of their own or if they are sessile (without a stem). You should also make a note of the veining of the leaf, and if the underside differs in colour and texture. Also check whether the plant is hairy or shiny. Try not to be inhibited about any lack of talent: the more you practise the better you will get. For equipment you will need a small box of water colour paints, a jar of water with a secure lid, a small pad of cartridge or water colour paper, pencils and a magnifying glass.

An artist's illustration showing a wild flower with detail drawings and notes.

Stinking Hellebore
(Helleborus foetidus)
2½ ft high
strong smelling
flowers often red
at edge of sepals
lower stem leaf
bract like upper
stem leaves paler
green and undivided
glossy
dark green
palmate leaves
stem leaf
cross section
of flower
petal-less
sepal
stamen

Flowers in art

Although cavemen often drew animals, they rarely included plants in their exquisite paintings. In fact, the earliest recorded example of serious botanical art can be seen in the bas-reliefs in the Great Temple of Karnak in Egypt which date back to 1500 BC (see below). However it was not until around the fourth century BC that the Greeks established botany as a science, and consequently plant illustration became more common.

As plants became familiar ingredients in medicine it was necessary to draw them with great accuracy, for the simple reason that two flowers may look alike, but one could contain a healing drug and the other a poison. Identification was therefore vital, and a finely detailed illustration a handy reference. The elder illustrated here is a good

An Egyptian bas-relief of water plants in the Great Temple of Karnak, 1500BC

Capital, Southwell Minster, late 13th century

Japanese painting of a Tree Paeony, on silk, 1854

example of a botanical drawing; the leaves of the plant are used for bruises and chilblains and the berries for a palatable wine.

Plants, however, have not always been illustrated accurately, and when drawings were copied for herbals the interpretations were sometimes less than skilful. Nevertheless, flowers have also been painted deliberately in a more stylized and impressionistic manner, often to emphasize beauty. The Japanese painting shown below is a good example, and no less attractive than a botanical drawing. Indeed flowers have made ideal subjects for purely decorative works, such as this impressive tile design by William Morris (see below). But for identification purposes there is no better reference than the carefully studied, life-like illustration.

The Elder has long been used in medicine and winemaking. To avoid unpleasant mistakes it was vital that drawings should be accurate and not stylized.

A design for tiles by William Morris, 1876

Conservation

Fifty years ago there used to be a small meadow in southern England that belonged to an old man who had one donkey. The meadow had not been ploughed for at least a century and it was seldom grazed even by the donkey. In summer it was a profusion of wild flowers, where small children could go and gather colourful nosegays to their hearts' content. All the fields around this one were green with grass and only a few flowers were growing here and there. No doubt by now the old man's meadow, in new hands, has been ploughed, sown with grass seed and treated with selective herbicides, and is now just a green pasture.

The story of this meadow could epitomize the history of the countryside during the last four or five hundred years. The increase in the human population, the need to grow more food, the use of herbicides, and pollution generally has robbed us of thousands and thousands of small meadows throughout the British Isles.

The ill-effects of pollution and of the misuse of herbicides are too well known to need further emphasis here. What is perhaps less generally appreciated is the way wholly laudable improvements in methods of agriculture have added to these ill-effects. Thus, the sowing of seed grain cleaned of weed seeds has increased the yield of grain per acre but has caused the loss of traditional inhabitants of the cornfields. No longer do we see fields scarlet with Poppies or blue with Cornflowers. Today the sight of the purple Corncockle or the Corn Marigold is rare indeed where once they were abundant.

Even more to blame for the disappearance of many flowers from the countryside are those who have selfishly culled whole plants from the wild. Picking the flowers is bad enough but digging them up by

the roots to take home and plant in the garden is far worse. The legislation protecting wild flowers may seem over-stringent but it came not a moment too soon. Laws not only serve as a deterrent; they also have the positive effect of making more and more people conservation conscious. Instead of picking flowers to take them home to identify, the habit is growing of taking the book to the flower for this purpose. People also look for ways to form sanctuaries for wild flowers; and when it becomes known that a locality containing rare plants is threatened by some industrial project or the like an informed band of sympathizers is there ready to protest.

In the last 300 years, 20 native species have become extinct in Britain, 12 in this century. More than 100 others are found in fewer than five small localities. The Lady's Slipper Orchid, for example, is now found in one locality only. Had nothing been done, some of our most beautiful or interesting flowers would by now be no more than names in books. Some of the main ravages have been checked and there is hope that the trend may be reversed.

How to use this book

In the following pages there are descriptions and illustrations of 160 wild flowers. Each double-page spread is devoted to two nearly related species, one the main subject, the other secondary. The main subject in each instance is illustrated by a large colour plate on the right-hand page. On the left-hand page, there is information about the history of the species, or outstanding facts about it, such as its use in medicine or commerce, in symbolism or folklore. Also included on this page is a summary of structural or other details that will help the beginner to learn what to look for in a plant, in order to identify it, and then to understand its way of life, where it is found, what time of year it blooms, and so on.

One important piece of information concerns the height to which the plant grows. Where the maximum height is given it should be remembered that the plant may be less than this height, often well below it, since plants vary in size according to the soil and situation.

Although the secondary species are dealt with less fully they do serve to give the reader a sense of relating species to each other in the broad scheme of classification. Unless otherwise stated this plant comes from the same family as the main subject.

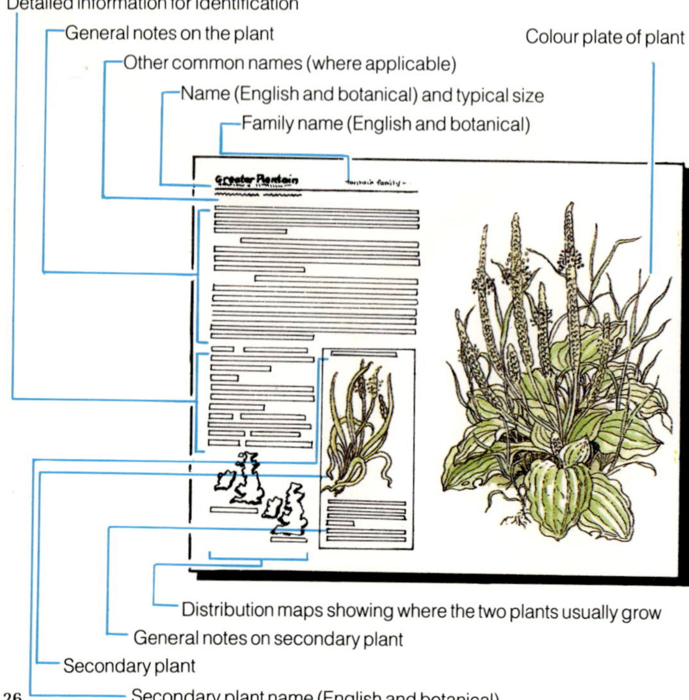

FIELD GUIDE
TO BRITISH
WILD
FLOWERS

Common Nettle

NETTLE FAMILY

Urtica dioica 30-150 cm (1-5 ft)

Urticaceae

Other name: Stinging Nettle

This is one plant everyone recognizes by its painful sting. It is a perennial which spreads by whitish underground shoots and swamps the vegetation around it. Although many plant-eating animals do not like it, it does provide food for the caterpillars of some of our most colourful butterflies, such as the peacock, small tortoiseshell and red admiral. Soup can be made with the young shoots or they can be stewed and eaten like spinach. The mature stems contain a fibre formerly used for weaving cloth. The stings are modified hairs coating the leaves. Each is hollow and ends in a small head strengthened by silica. When touched, however lightly, this breaks off and penetrates the skin. At the same time a fluid flows from it containing histamine and other substances which produce a skin rash. Traditionally, this can be treated by rubbing with a dock leaf which has been shown to contain an antidote to the histamine.

Habitat: Waste places, hedges, woods, pastures.
Flowers: June-September, hanging or spreading, green, in tassel-like clusters up to 10 cm (4 in) long, plants one-sexed.
Stem: Erect, hairy.
Leaves: Heart-shaped, stalked, with toothed edges, in opposite pairs with four stipules at each node.
Fruit: A small achene.

Mistletoe up to 100 cm (39 in)
Viscum album

From the family *Loranthaceae*, Mistletoe is an evergreen shrub parasitic on branches of a wide range of deciduous trees, sometimes on conifers. It is a close relative of the nettle, and long used in religious and amorous symbolism. Flowers are single-sexed and the berries poisonous.

Common Sorrel

DOCK FAMILY

Rumex acetosa 30-100 cm (12-39 in)

Polygonaceae

Other names: Sour Leaves, Sour Dock

The Common Sorrel is an acid-tasting perennial with a high Vitamin C content and it is used as a vegetable, either cooked or in salads. In quantity, however, it is harmful as it contains oxalic acid. The stems are erect and the plants are mainly single-sexed, most of them bearing male flowers only with six stamens, or female flowers only with three carpels. Both male and female flowers may, however, be found on the same plant. The flowers are wind-pollinated. The seeds are dispersed in large numbers in cattle dung, and tests have shown that such seeds have a high rate of germination. Its other method of reproduction, troublesome when the plant is in your garden, is by persistent rootstock. The name 'sorrel' is from the Old French meaning 'reddish'.

Habitat: Dry grasslands especially, also woods.
Flowers: May-August, small, lacking petals, with six sepals in two whorls, green tinged with red.
Stem: Erect, hairless.
Leaves: Arrow-shaped with basal lobes projecting backwards, arranged alternately on the stems.
Fruit: A triangular nut which becomes enclosed in the sepals that enlarge after fertilization.

Common Sorrel

Knotgrass

Knotgrass up to 200 cm (80 in)
Polygonum aviculare

Knotgrass is an inconspicuous annual weed of both cultivated ground and waste places. It varies in form, sometimes trailing, sometimes erect, with solitary, very small green flowers with white or pink margins. As in other members of the dock family a sheath at the leaf base forms a partial tube, the ochrea, around the stem.

Fat-hen

GOOSEFOOT FAMILY
Chenopodiaceae

Chenopodium album 10-90 cm (4-36 in)

Other names: White Goosefoot, Dirty Dick

The origin of the name 'Fat-hen' is unknown. It seems to have come into use as late as the end of the 18th century, although it is a very common weed. *Chenopodium* comes from two Greek words, *cheno*, a goose and *podion*, a small foot, and alludes to the shape of the leaf. Fat-hen, although a troublesome annual on broken ground, has no creeping roots or underground stems and is easily eradicated. Well-grown plants are like a pyramid in shape and are covered with a white mealy powder. The flowers, individually inconspicuous, are borne in dense spikes. Very young plants covered with dew tend to have a mauve 'bloom', especially on the undersides of the leaves. The young tender shoots used to be eaten like spinach.

Habitat: Prolific in gardens, also on cultivated ground, waysides and waste places.
Flowers: June-October, bisexual, greenish, perianth in 2-5 parts, 1-5 stamens, usually two stigmas on a single-chambered ovary.
Stem: Hairless, erect, often reddish.
Leaves: Variable, lanceolate to diamond-shaped, lower leaves toothed.
Fruit: Single-seeded nut.

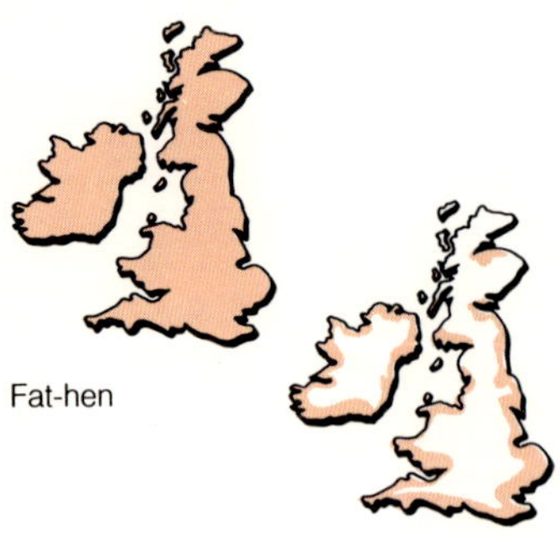

Fat-hen

Sea Beet

Sea Beet 30-120 cm (1-4 ft)
Beta vulgaris subsp. *maritima*

The Sea Beet is a reminder that several members of the *Chenopodiaceae* are plants of economic importance. These include the beet, spinach, orache and the manglewurzel or mangold. Sea Beet which may be annual grows on the seashore, above high-tide mark, and lacks the swollen tap root of its cultivated relatives.

Glasswort

GOOSEFOOT FAMILY
Chenopodiaceae

Salicornia europaea 15-45 cm (6-18 in)

Other names: Sea Samphire, Jointed Glasswort

The scientific name of this annual (from Latin *sal*, salt and *cornu*, horn) derives from the places where it is found and its antler-like form. Glasswort has also been described as resembling a small, multi-branched cactus, and like a cactus it does, in fact, need to regulate its water supply. However, in a cactus the stem alone is swollen and the leaves reduced to spines, but in the Glasswort the stem and leaves are both swollen, and together give the plant a succulent appearance. The flowers are tiny and in groups of three. Each flower is made up of two stamens and a very short style bearing a cross-cleft stigma. The fleshy, jointed stems are normally branched but may be unbranched.

Habitat: Salt marshes, sometimes on the seashore or on sand inland.
Flowers: August-September, difficult to see, in clusters of three, arranged in triangles, green with yellow stamens and enclosed in fleshy bracts.
Stem: Jointed.
Leaves: Fleshy, in opposite pairs, wrapped so closely around the stem as to appear absent.
Fruit: A dry, one-seeded nut.

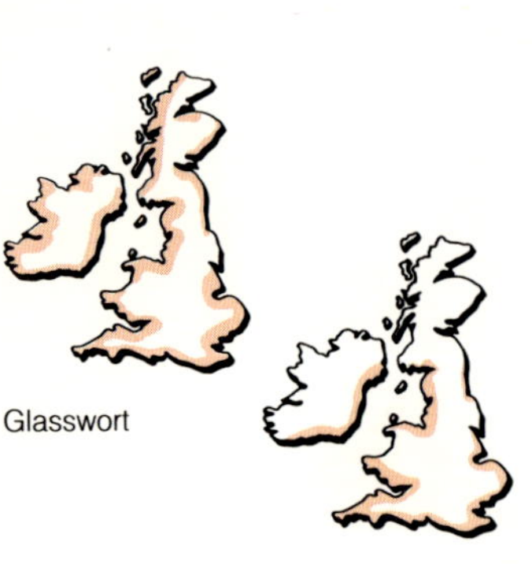

Glasswort

Sea-purslane

Sea-purslane up to 150 cm (60 in)
Halimione portulacoides

The Sea-purslane is nearly related to the Glasswort and, like it, lives in salt marshes, but it may also form dense mats on the seashore. It is a small shrubby annual rooted in the mud and has woody stems and fleshy, silvery-white, mealy leaves, oblong to oval in shape. Its spikes of small, single-sexed flowers have few branches.

Bladder Campion

Silene vulgaris 60-90 cm (2-3 ft)

PINK FAMILY
Caryophyllaceae

Other name: White Bottle

The outstanding feature of this perennial is its bladder-like calyx. It can also be easily identified by the way the individual flowers droop, by the greyish foliage and by the fact that the lower leaves wither before the blooms appear. The nectaries are deep in the tube formed by the petals, well down in the calyx so that only long-tongued, night-flying moths can reach them. From a stout rootstock the branches rise giving off a pair of leaves at each joint. There has been much speculation as to whether the Bladder Campion and the Sea Campion, shown below, are one and the same species, but it now seems certain that they represent two distinct species and that the Bladder Campion arrived from Europe after the Ice Age had ended, whereas the Sea Campion was here during the Ice Age.

Habitat: Grassy places, cultivated and waste ground, especially on limy soils.
Flowers: May-September, white, five petals deeply cleft, sepals form a bladder with 20 netted veins.
Stem: Erect, hairless, greyish.
Leaves: Pointed oval, edges often wavy, opposite.
Fruit: Globose capsule opening by six small teeth at the top.

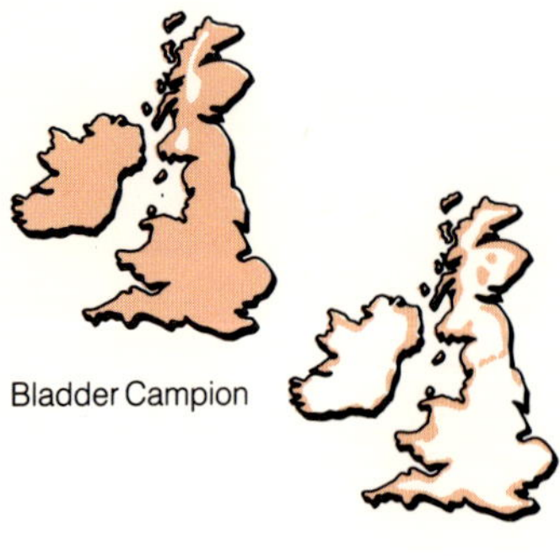

Bladder Campion

Sea Campion

Sea Campion 8-25 cm (3-10 in)
Silene maritima

The Sea Campion could be mistaken for a dwarf variety of the Bladder Campion, and it has often been treated as a subspecies of it. It is a mat-forming, low-growing perennial common near the seashore and on cliffs as well as by the sides of mountain streams, flowering throughout the summer.

Red Campion

Silene dioica 30-90 cm (1-3 ft)

PINK FAMILY
Caryophyllaceae

Other names: Red Robin, Bridget in her Bravery

The Red Campion is biennial to perennial with long slender stems, erect but tending to 'flop' unless supported by other vegetation. The branching of its shoots is typical of the family. Each main stem ends in a red flower, but just below this flower are two buds opposite each other which grow out to form oblique branches, also ending in a flower, and this again has one or two buds just below it. The flowers are single-sexed and borne on separate plants. The petals are heart-shaped with a deep cleft. The male flower has five stamens; the female flower has five carpels fused to form a single-chambered ovary bearing five conspicuous free styles. The Red Campion is one of several plants, including the Bluebell and the Wood Anemone, known as Cuckooflowers in addition to the member of the family *Cruciferae* accepted here as the Cuckooflower.

Habitat: Woods, hedges, on cliffs, especially near shade, in rich soils.
Flowers: March-November, bright red to pink, with five cleft petals in a globose, toothed calyx, stamens and pistils in separate flowers.
Stem: Irregularly erect, softly hairy.
Leaves: Pointed oval, lower leaves stalked.
Fruit: Globose seed-pod with ten apical teeth which roll back.

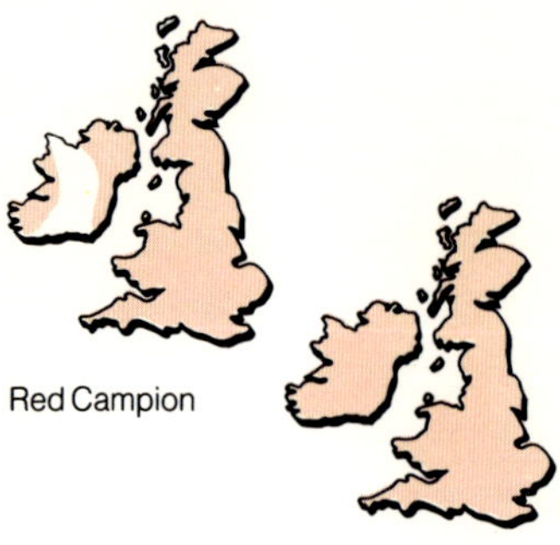

Red Campion

Ragged-Robin

Ragged-Robin 30-75 cm (12-29 in)
Lychnis flos-cuculi

The Ragged-Robin has fundamentally the same form as the Red Campion and it also has red flowers. The obvious difference between the two is that the petals of the former look ragged and tattered. The Ragged-Robin, a perennial, grows in damp meadows and marshes.

Common Chickweed

Stellaria media up to 90 cm (3 ft)

PINK FAMILY
Caryophyllaceae

Other names: Adder's Meat, Satin Flower

Common Chickweed, if undisturbed, can form attractive low-growing masses. It is a nuisance in gardens but much relished by birds, whether wild or caged – hence its name. An annual, it sends out numerous delicate branches over the soil covered with bright green, succulent, oval leaves arranged on the stems in pairs. Down each internode on the stems runs a single line of small white hairs, the lines on two consecutive internodes alternating. The parts of each small flower are in fives or multiples of five, with five small green sepals, five white petals each deeply cloven giving a star-like effect. The flowers are open from 9 am until noon, but if it rains they remain closed. Formerly chickweed was used as a pot herb and a table vegetable.

Habitat: Cultivated and waste ground.
Flowers: All the year, small, white numerous with deep-lobed violet petals, shorter or little longer than the sepals, 3-10 stamens.
Stem: Weak, straggling, with single line of hairs down stem.
Leaves: Oval with a sharp point, upper leaves stalkless, lower leaves long-stemmed.
Fruit: A capsule containing small seeds which splits into as many valves as there are styles.

Greater Stitchwort 15-60 cm
Stellaria holostea (6-24 in)

The Greater Stitchwort is a perennial of the woods and hedgerows, usually on heavy soils. Its flowers of dazzling white may be seen from April to August. Each flower has five sepals, five deeply cloven petals with pronounced greenish veins, ten stamens and three styles. Its slender stems are easily broken at the nodes.

Meadow Buttercup

BUTTERCUP FAMILY

Ranunculus acris 30-90 cm (1-3 ft)

Ranunculaceae

Other names: Butterflower, Gold-cup, Meadow Crowfoot, Upright Crowfoot

Buttercups and Daisies are inseparable in our minds, although the former are flamboyantly conspicuous in meadows whereas the Daisies score by sheer numbers. More so formerly than today, during summer the pastures are sprinkled with the golden flowers of the Meadow Buttercup. Yet the plant, a perennial, is normally carefully avoided by livestock because its sap contains an acrid substance poisonous to cattle. In humans this irritating substance (protoanemonine) can cause unpleasant blistering to sensitive skins. Cattle have been known to eat it if let into fields when especially hungry, and they then suffer from inflammation of the lining of the mouth. The name, originally used in the plural only, did not come into use until the end of the 18th century. Before that the plant was known as Butterflower.

Habitat: Meadows, damp grassy places.
Flowers: April-September, yellow with five erect greenish sepals, five petals, numerous stamens and many carpels arranged spirally on a receptacle.
Stem: Hairy, not furrowed, branching.
Leaves: Basal leaves on long stalks, with sheathing bases, blade divided into 3-7 lobes with coarsely toothed margins.
Fruit: A collection of achenes each with a short 'beak'.

Meadow Buttercup

Creeping Buttercup

Creeping Buttercup 15-30 cm
Ranunculus repens (6-12 in)

The perennial Creeping Buttercup has the general appearance of the Meadow Buttercup but it is not as tall, about 30 cm (1 ft) with stouter, furrowed stems that creep over the ground throwing out roots at each node, making it an unmitigated pest in gardens and difficult to eradicate successfully.

Marsh-marigold

BUTTERCUP FAMILY
Ranunculaceae

Caltha palustris 5-60 cm (2-24 in)

Other name: Kingcup

There is no grander sight in May than a marsh covered with the golden flowers of the Marsh-marigold, especially when bathed in sunshine. It is no surprise therefore that this perennial is such a favourite and this is reflected in the many common names it has been given – Golden Cup, Soldier's Button, May-blobs, Mare-blob, Horse-blob, Brave Celandine, Mary-bud, Publicans and Sinners. In Scotland it is known as Luckan Gowan. The reason for some of these names is not easy to comprehend or indeed why 'marigold' (i.e. Mary's gold, a reference to the Blessed Virgin) should have become attached to it since it bears little resemblance to the familiar marigold and no relationship to it.

Habitat: Marshes and wet places.
Flowers: March-August, golden yellow, with five yellow sepals (there is disagreement as to whether they are sepals or petals).
Stem: Fleshy, hollow, shiny, springing from a thick creeping rootstock.
Leaves: Basal leaves stalked, kidney-shaped, shiny, margins toothed, upper leaves small, almost stalkless.
Fruit: Green pods which split to release their seeds.

Marsh-marigold

Wood Anemone

Wood Anemone 6-30 cm
Anemone nemorosa (2½-12 in)

The Wood Anemone or Wind Flower is a spring flower, but more delicate than the Marsh-marigold. Also a perennial, it has a creeping rootstock from which arise separately the stalked white flowers subtended by three deeply divided leaves. The foliage leaves, which spring direct from the rootstock, are similar in shape.

Common Water-crowfoot

BUTTERCUP FAMILY

Ranunculus aquatilis 1.5 m (5 ft) long

Ranunculaceae

Other name: Water Crowfoot

The principal interest of the Common Water-crowfoot, annual to perennial and a typical member of the Buttercup family, is in its leaves. Those floating on the surface are borne on long stalks. They are trilobed with each of the lobes divided into smaller lobes. The submerged leaves are finely divided, almost hair-like, allowing water to flow freely over and around them, the slender subdivisions enabling them to absorb more oxygen from the water than would be the case with more normal leaves. The floating leaves serve, in addition to their usual function of manufacturing food, to buoy up the end branches of the stems that bear the flowers, so keeping the flowers above the surface of the water.

Habitat: Still or slow-flowing water to 1 m (3 ft) deep.
Flowers: May-August, Buttercup-like but white tinted with yellow, made up of five sepals, five petals and numerous stamens and carpels.
Stem: Branching, mainly underwater.
Leaves: Of two kinds; floating leaves trilobed, submerged leaves finely divided.
Fruit: Group of one-seeded carpels each with a persistent style.

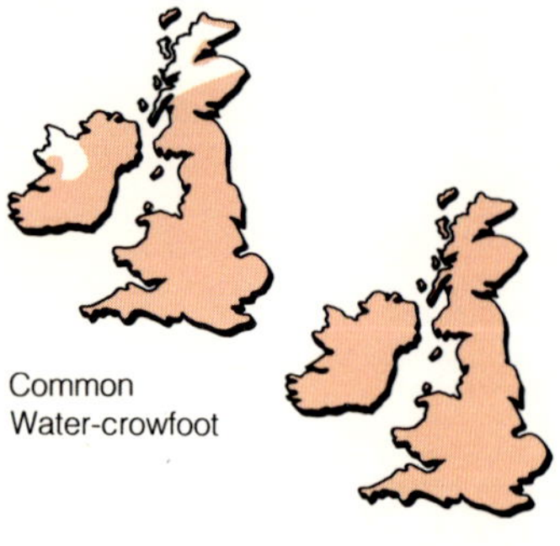

Common Water-crowfoot

Lesser Celandine

Lesser Celandine 5-25 cm
Ranunculus ficaria (2-10 in)

The Lesser Celandine or Pilewort can be a nuisance in a garden but its natural habitat is woods and hedge banks. A low-growing herb with dark green, fleshy heart-shaped leaves, its golden yellow star-like flowers have 8-12 narrow petals which go whitish with age. Its base bears a cluster of tuber-like bulbils.

Common Poppy

Papaver rhoeas up to 60 cm (2 ft)

POPPY FAMILY
Papaveraceae

Other names: Field Poppy, Corn Poppy, Red Poppy, Corn Rose

The annual Common Poppy, symbol of fertility and, since World War 1, of sacrifice, is almost too familiar to need description, although, in fact, today it is something of a rarity. Its scarlet petals have a velvety look. The two sepals drop as the bud opens, and the petals fall as soon as the flower is pollinated. At the centre of the flower are numerous black stamens surrounding a single-chambered ovary The Common Poppy reached Great Britain from the Near East soon after the Ice Age ended. It contains a poisonous alkaloid, yet its petals have been used to make a cough mixture and as a substitute for tea. Although one plant can yield 50,000 seeds, improved methods of cleaning grain have led to the poppy's disappearance from cornfields.

Habitat: Fields, cultivated ground, wasteland.
Flowers: May-August, large, scarlet, four petals within two green sepals, petals crumpled in the bud, often with black basal blotch.
Stem: Upright, with spreading hairs.
Leaves: Once or twice pinnate with coarsely toothed, narrow, fine-pointed segments.
Fruit: Large rounded 'pepperpot' capsule ribbed on the sides and with a distinct lid with radial ridges.

Common Poppy

Greater Celandine

Greater Celandine 30-90 cm (1-3 ft)
Chelidonium majus

The Greater Celandine is not even remotely related to the Lesser Celandine. It is a perennial with golden yellow flowers, up to 90 cm (3 ft) high, growing in hedges and on wasteland. Its leaves are pinnate with five to seven lobed or toothed leaflets. Its sap is orange-coloured and oozes when a stem is snapped.

Shepherd's-purse

CABBAGE FAMILY

Capsella bursa-pastoris 15-60 cm (6-24 in) *Cruciferae*

Other names: Common Shepherd's Purse, Pickpocket

A very common inhabitant of bare or broken ground, Shepherd's-purse can be a pest in the garden although its natural habitat is waste places and tracksides. A variable species, annual or biennial, it does not thrive among grass or other dense vegetation. Its lower leaves form a rosette hugging the surface of the soil, and from this spring tall slender stems, only slightly branching, which bear spikes of small white flowers. Each flower has four petals and four sepals forming a cross, as in wallflowers and cresses, and cultivated plants such as cabbage, turnip and radish. Shepherd's-purse itself is edible and was formerly used as a pot herb although it has a slightly pungent taste. Its seed-pods are heart-shaped capsules resembling the pouches peasants used to wear to carry their food in.

Habitat: Bare ground, waste places.
Flowers: All the year except for late December to early January, small, white.
Stem: Erect, with or without hairs.
Leaves: Basal leaves pinnate, deeply lobed, upper leaves entire, clasping, lanceolate.
Fruit: Pod an inverted heart-shape.

Shepherd's-purse

Cuckooflower

Cuckooflower 15-60 cm (6-24 in)
Cardamine pratensis

The Cuckooflower grows up to 60 cm (2 ft) tall and blooms from April until June. Its cruciform flowers are white or pale lilac. It is a perennial and may be found in marshes and damp meadows. Alternative names are Lady's Smock, Milkmaids and Meadow Bitter-cress. The Cuckooflower is edible and may be used in salads.

Navelwort

STONECROP FAMILY

Umbilicus rupestris 10-40 cm (4-16 in) *Crassulaceae*

Other names: Pennywort, Wall Pennywort, Kidneywort

There is something elegantly charming about the perennial Navelwort with its neatly circular leaves and, more especially, its tall spikes of delicate drooping green to white bells. The whole plant is fleshy and succulent. The leaves, alternately arranged, have long fleshy stalks. Their blades are round and thick, slightly cup-shaped with a wavy margin. The leaves have been nicknamed penny pies. In old medicinal herbals, Navelwort was recommended for treating scalds and burns; its juice was also said to have soothing properties and was used to relieve such complaints as chilblains and inflammation. It can be seen most frequently in western England, but is rare in eastern and northern England and Scotland.

Habitat: Rocks, banks, walls, crevices, not on limy soil.
Flowers: June-August, greenish or pinkish-white, pendulous bell-shaped, toothed, in spikes.
Stem: Rounded, smooth, erect, usually unbranched.
Leaves: Rounded, fleshy, with a 'navel' at the centre.
Fruit: Star-shaped, formed of several carpels.

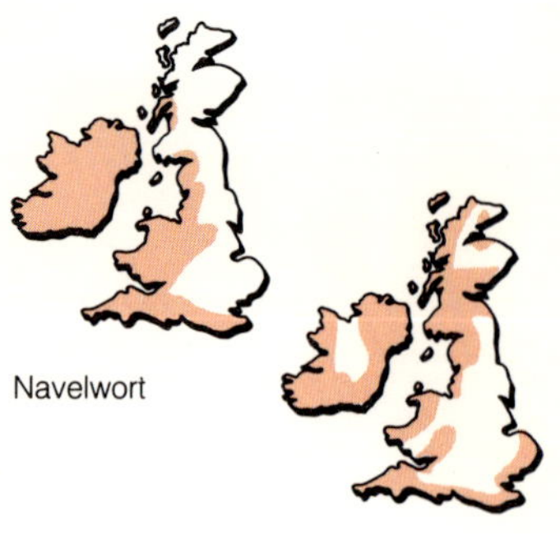

English Stonecrop 2-5 cm (¾-2 in)
Sedum anglicum

The English Stonecrop is found in rocky coastal areas, forming low, perennial, evergreen mats, its leaves fleshy and green but reddening with age. It flowers from June to August or September; its tiny blooms are white tinged with pink below. The cylindrical leaves are water-storage organs enabling the plant to grow in dry places.

Meadow Saxifrage

Saxifraga granulata up to 50 cm (20 in)

SAXIFRAGE FAMILY
Saxifragaceae

Unlike the rock-loving saxifrages, the leaves of the Meadow Saxifrage are not fleshy. This, together with its non-rocky habitat, tends to belie its name, which is from the Latin, *saxum*, rock, and *frangere*, to break. A special feature of this perennial is that it multiplies from season to season by means of tuber-like bulbils grouped in a cluster at the base of the stem. These are brown and hidden in the soil and it is because they look like grains that the species is named *granulata*. One peculiarity of the Meadow Saxifrage is that the stamens ripen before the stigmas. Another is that the central flower of each cluster opens first and differs markedly from the other flowers in the cluster in having large fat stigmas, borne on long styles and covered with pimples. The stigmas are especially noticeable after the stamens have shed their pollen, and should be looked for in identifying the plant.

Habitat: Grasslands, margins of woods, dry places.
Flowers: April-June, small white, in loose clusters.
Stem: Erect, little branched.
Leaves: Kidney-shaped, slightly lobed, mainly at base of stem.
Fruit: Capsule formed of two carpels fused below and more or less free above.

Round-leaved Sundew 6-25 cm
Drosera rotundifolia (2½-10 in)

The Round-leaved Sundew (from the family *Droseraceae*), also known as the Common Sundew, is a perennial that traps insects with sticky club-shaped tentacles on its leaves. The tentacles then give out a digestive juice which dissolves the hard parts of the insect and the 'soup' so formed is absorbed into the leaf to nourish the plant.

Meadowsweet

ROSE FAMILY
Rosaceae

Filipendula ulmaria 60-120 cm (2-4 ft)

Other names: Bridewort, Meadwort, Queen of the Meadow

Conspicuous for its creamy-white, flattish heads of small massed, sweetly scented blossoms, the perennial Meadowsweet attracts numerous insects by its perfume but has no nectaries. In the days when rushes were laid on the floors of houses and soiled by the excrement of household dogs and mouldering scraps of food, Meadowsweet was strewn on the rushes to counteract the odour. It was also infused in mead, the popular drink, to give additional flavour. One of the most attractive of our wild flowers, Meadowsweet is often given the scientific name *Spiraea* in books. This name is also used, quite erroneously, by gardeners for a common greenhouse plant, which should more properly be called *Astilbe*. The confusion thus caused is best resolved by using the name *Filipendula* for the Queen of the Meadow.

Habitat: Damp meadows, riversides, damp ground generally.
Flowers: June-September, small, white or cream, in dense terminal inflorescences.
Stem: Tall, erect, stiff.
Leaves: Divided into toothed leaflets between which smaller leaflets are interspersed, downy on undersides.
Fruit: A collection of splitting follicles.

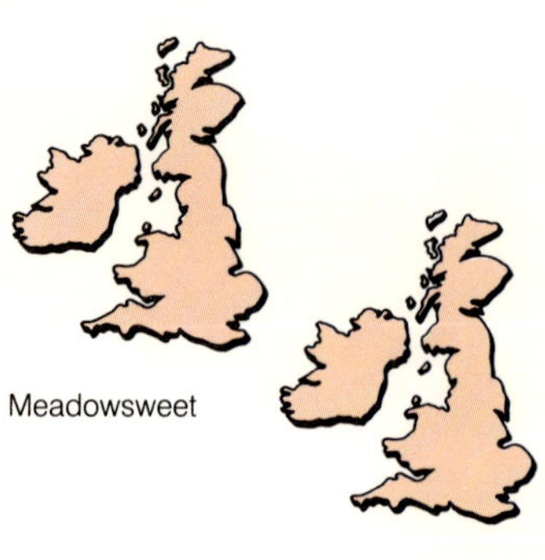

Meadowsweet

Bramble

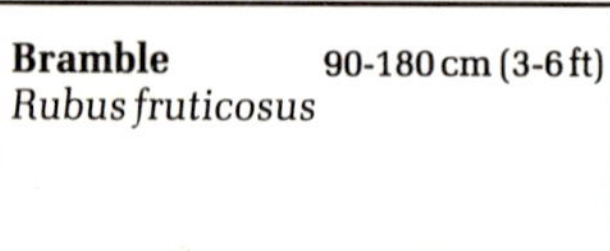

Bramble 90-180 cm (3-6 ft)
Rubus fruticosus

Whether known as Bramble or Blackberry the angled prickly stems of this perennial and the fruits are as well known and common as any wild plant.
A very variable species, some 2,000 microspecies have been recognized. The fruit is green at first, turning to red and finally blackish-purple, Aug to Oct.

Barren Strawberry

Potentilla sterilis 5-15 cm (2-6 in)

ROSE FAMILY
Rosaceae

Other name: Strawberry-leaved Cinquefoil

A small perennial with hairs on the stems and leaves, the entire plant spreads low over the ground. The name, Barren Strawberry, is misleading for, although it does not produce fleshy fruits like the Wild Strawberry, the plant is far from barren or sterile. In some ways the alternative common name is to be preferred, for it indicates the relationship to the cinquefoils. The Barren Strawberry is one of the earliest flowers to bloom, often in January, but it may not be noticed because of its lack of conspicuous blossoms. The Barren Strawberry and Wild Strawberry are rather similar in general appearance, except for the long thin runners in the latter. Even without the fruits, however, it is possible to distinguish between the two by the flowers. In the Barren Strawberry the petals have obvious gaps between them, while in the fuller flowers of the Wild Strawberry the petals touch.

Habitat: Dry grasslands, open woods, hedgerows.
Flowers: February-May, small, white, with gaps between the slightly notched petals, on low stems.
Stem: Forming runners.
Leaves: Trefoil, leaflets with toothed margins.
Fruit: Dry, not strawberry-like, a collection of achenes.

Silverweed up to 80 cm (32 in)
Potentilla anserina

Silverweed is a creeping perennial on dry, rocky ground. Its fern-like, downy leaves are divided into six to eight pairs of leaflets with one at the end, all with deeply toothed margins. The golden-yellow flowers appear from June to August. Its runners often invade the surfaces of little-used roads.

Tormentil

ROSE FAMILY

Potentilla erecta 10-50 cm (4-20 in)

Rosaceae

Other name: Common Tormentil

Tormentil is a slender perennial with a woody rootstock sending up erect flowering shoots. Its name is said to be the diminutive of *tormentum*, Latin for pain, and its rootstock was formerly used in the treatment of dysentery. Its main peculiarities are in its flowers and its stem leaves. The yellow flowers have only four petals instead of the five typical for the family and the four sepals make the shape of a cross. At the centre is a mass of orange-yellow anthers. The stem leaves are stalkless and appear to have five leaflets because of their two conspicuous leaf-like stipules. The root is peculiar. It is thick, brown and finger-shaped but pink inside.

Habitat: Moors, heaths, bogs and grassy places, in woods and on mountains, not on limy soils.
Flowers: May-September, yellow, in loose heads, long-stalked.
Stem: A stout woody stock.
Leaves: Basal leaves long-stalked with three oval coarsely toothed leaflets.
Fruit: Groups of dry achenes on a dome-shaped receptacle.

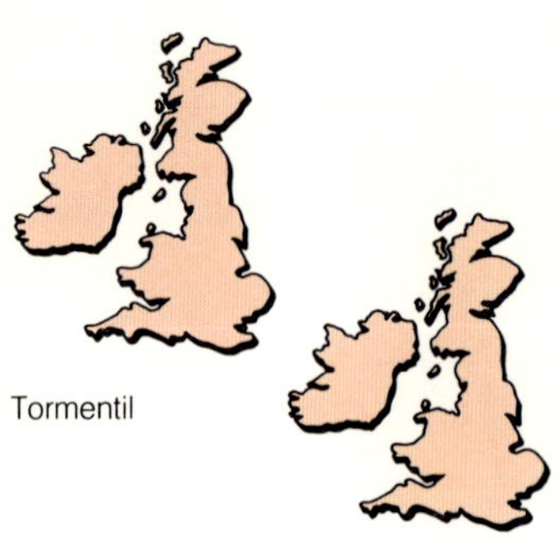

Tormentil

Wild Strawberry

Wild Strawberry 5-15 cm (2-6 in)
Fragaria vesca

The fruits of the Wild Strawberry are fleshy red receptacles, small versions of the familiar cultivated strawberry, which derived from it. The plant flowers from May to July, the ripe fruits being present in June and July. It is a perennial of open woods and hedge banks.

Wood Avens

ROSE FAMILY
Rosaceae

Geum urbanum up to 60 cm (2 ft)

Other names: Common Avens, Herb Bennet

The Wood Avens might pass unnoticed except that its hooked fruits are so frequently found clinging to our clothes. The name Avens is from the Latin *avens*, or oat, and refers to the awns, the spike-like bristles found on oats and barley. The fruits of the Wood Avens are achenes, each of which has an awn at the end with a double-curved kink halfway up. When the fruit ripens the outer portion of the awn is shed leaving a hook, like an old-fashioned buttonhook in shape. This attaches itself to clothing or the fur of animals, a means of dispersing its seeds. The generic name *Geum* is from the Greek for 'taste' because the roots have an aromatic flavour, those of the water avens, for example, tasting like cocoa. Herb Bennet is a corruption of *herba benedicta*, an allusion to this perennial plant's supposed medicinal properties.

Habitat: Woods, thickets, hedgerows, and shady places generally.
Flowers: May-September, sparse, yellow, erect in a loose inflorescence.
Stem: Erect, slender, downy, simple, bearing leaf-like stipules.
Leaves: Basal leaves pinnate with two or three pairs of oval, toothed leaflets and a larger terminal leaflet.
Fruit: A group of carpels with long hooked styles.

Wood Avens

Agrimony

Agrimony 30-60 cm (1-2 ft)
Agrimonia eupatoria

The Agrimony is another plant with seeds adapted to dispersal by animals. It is a leafy perennial with tall spikes of yellow flowers from June to September and markedly pinnate leaves. The apex of its grooved fruits is covered with small hooks.

Lady's-mantle

Alchemilla vulgaris 5-45 cm (2-18 in)

ROSE FAMILY
Rosaceae

Other name: Common Lady's Mantle

This is a perennial with erect or spreading stems and very small greenish-yellow flowers much used in herbal remedies in the past. Its generic name is, however, from the Arabic *alkemelych*, for alchemists collected the dew they needed for their experiments from these plants. So many of the more romantic flower names seem to have originated during the 16th century and Lady's-mantle is one of them, although it is not clear whether 'Lady' refers to women in general or to Our Lady. The former seems more likely. The dew was much sought after by ladies of fashion as a cosmetic, for its alleged power to give a delicate skin, remove freckles or even banish wrinkles. Because it was used by alchemists, it also had a reputation for possessing magical properties.

Habitat: Damp meadows, open woods, grassy and rocky places.
Flowers: May-September, tiny greenish-yellow.
Stem: Erect or spreading, from a woody rootstock.
Leaves: Basal leaves rounded, green on both sides, long-stalked, palmate, 5-11 lobed to half the width of the blade, margins toothed.
Fruit: Groups of carpels with long, free, persistent hooked styles.

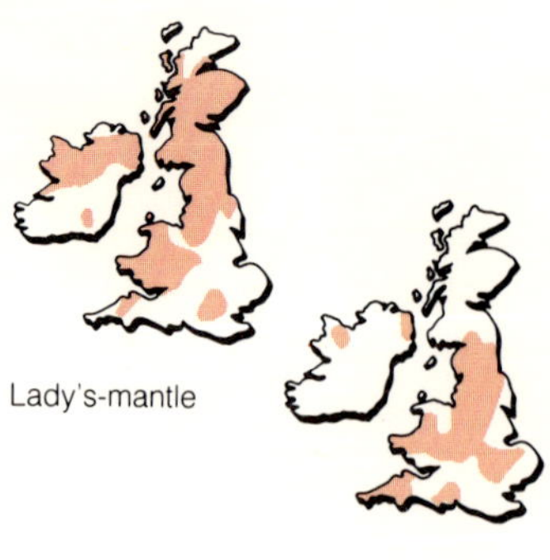

Lady's-mantle

Great Burnet

Great Burnet up to 1 m (3 ft)
Sanguisorba officinalis

The Great Burnet is a large perennial found growing up to 1 m (3 ft) high, especially in moist meadows. Its leaves are pinnate, the flowers tiny but massed into dense, rounded red heads. 'Burnet' is the Old French diminutive of brown which, 500 years later, was converted to brunette, a woman with brown hair.

Burnet Rose

ROSE FAMILY
Rosaceae

Rosa pimpinellifolia 10-100 cm (4-39 in)

Other name: Scotch Rose

The garden rose was the first to be cultivated, with the Romans bringing the cult of rose gardens to Britain. The Burnet Rose is perhaps, by a very narrow margin, the most attractive of our four species of wild roses, the others being the Dog, Field and Downy Roses, all perennials. It is low-growing, and its white fragrant blossoms contrast with the rich green of its foliage. The purplish black hips are brown before they ripen fully which gave this rose the name 'Burnet', meaning brown (see Great Burnet, page 64). The Burnet Rose is far from common in the south of Britain, hence its other name, Scotch Rose. Another marked feature is the numerous slender spines on the stems and these gave rise to the plant's earlier scientific name, *Rosa spinosissima*.

Habitat: Rocks, dunes, clifftops, often near the sea.
Flowers: May-July, white, sometimes pink.
Stem: Suckering, with numerous thorns and bristles.
Leaves: With small, rounded leaflets, conspicuously saw-toothed at the margins.
Fruit: Purple to black hips with the remains of sepals prominent on them.

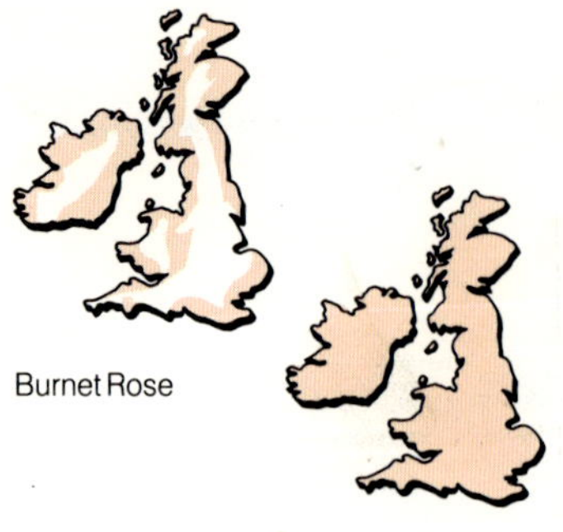

Burnet Rose

Dog Rose

Dog Rose 100-300 cm (39-120 in)
Rosa canina

By contrast, the Dog Rose, with its 3 m (10 ft) arching stems and pink to white flowers, is far more common in the south than the Burnet Rose. Its hips have been used as a source of Vitamin C since Neolithic times and are still used to make rosehip syrup and jam. They contain eight times as much Vitamin C as oranges.

Common Restharrow

Ononis repens 30-60 cm (1-2 ft)

PEA FAMILY
Leguminosae

Other name: Restharrow

The pink blossoms of the Restharrow stand out conspicuously on moors and clifftops. A perennial species, it either forms bushy growths or extensive mats, with the stems spreading and rooting at the nodes. The stems are woody, the roots long and tough, and the plant is not easy to remove from the ground; hence its name, since one meaning of 'rest' is to stop or arrest. Obviously our forebears were less impressed by the beauty of the plant than by the nuisance it caused when a piece of ground had to be cleared for cultivation or harrowed. Restharrow is also one of the plants with a fragrance which attracts insects but lacks nectaries to reward them for their visits.

Habitat: Dry pastures, uncultivated sandy places.
Flowers: June-September, pink, wings as long as the keel.
Stem: Spreading, with stolons, rooting, hairy, sometimes with a few soft spines.
Leaves: Trifoliate, but simple higher up the stem.
Fruit: Pods, small, with only a few seeds.

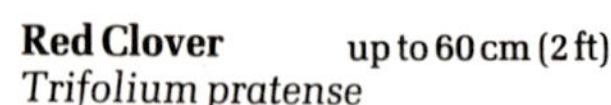

Red Clover up to 60 cm (2 ft)
Trifolium pratense

In some places in Britain the Red Clover or Purple Clover is known as Honeysuckle because of its copious supply of nectar in the dense flowerheads. The nectar is, however, deep in a tube formed by the petals and therefore only available to long-tongued bees, such as the bumblebee. Red Clover, a perennial, is a first-class fodder crop.

Common Bird's-foot-trefoil

PEA FAMILY
Leguminosae

Lotus corniculatus 10-40 cm (4-16 in)

Other names: Bacon and Eggs, Tom Thumb, Fingers and Thumb, Shoes and Stockings

This common perennial has enjoyed a wide popularity, judging by the many homely names it has received. It is also the Tufted Crow-toe of Milton's *Lycidas*. Another name is the Bird's Foot Lotus which has nothing to do with the well-known Lotus nor with the lotus-eaters, and its generic name is from the Greek *lotos* meaning three-leaved. Bird's-foot-trefoil commonly grows among grass, its blooms appearing as patches of yellow among the green, its own foliage partly hidden by the taller grasses. The flower has the typical pea family structure but the two petals forming the keel are united above and below leaving only a small opening at the apex. The pollen is shed before the bud opens. Five of the stamens then swell and push the pollen through this opening on to the stigma, so effecting self-pollination.

Habitat: Grassy places, fields, meadows, verges.
Flowers: May-September, yellow tinted orange or red. 5-7 in a head on a long stalk.
Stem: Procumbent, downy or, more usually, hairless.
Leaves: With five leaflets, the lower two bent back so that the leaf appears trefoil.
Fruit: Straight pods looking like the toes of a bird.

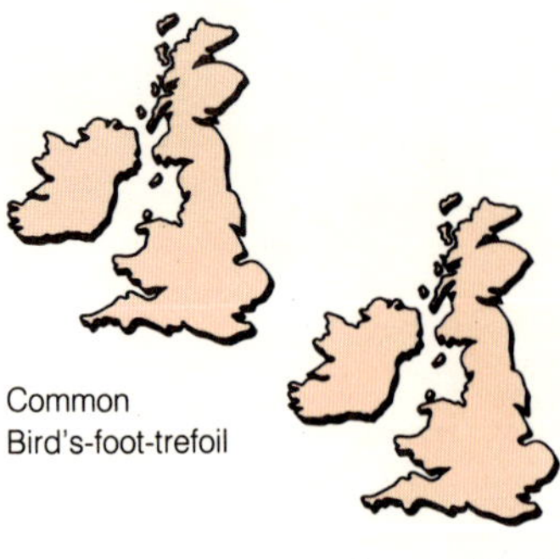

Common Bird's-foot-trefoil

Common Vetch

Common Vetch 15-120 cm (6-48 in)
Vicia sativa

The Common Vetch grows among grass or on arable land but especially near hedges, clambering up stouter plants. An annual, its leaves are made up of four to seven pairs of leaflets, its flowers the usual 'pea blossom', reddish, violet or purple.

Wood-sorrel

WOOD-SORREL FAMILY

Oxalis acetosella 8-15 cm (3-6 in)

Oxalidaceae

Other names: Common Wood-sorrel, Alleluia, Green Sauce, Stubwort, Woodsour, Wood-sower

When a wild plant has numerous common names the chances are that it formerly had medicinal uses. Wood-sorrel, a perennial, is no exception. It was not only used medicinally, but also included in salads although sparingly because in quantity it can be poisonous as it contains oxalic acid. The trefoil leaves are sensitive to light and temperature and close up at night and during dull weather. Each flower, on its long stalk, has five sepals and five petals, ten stamens and five carpels. The fruit is a capsule with elastic walls and when ripe it turns inside-out suddenly, catapulting the seeds some distance from the parent plant.

Habitat: Woods and other shady places.
Flowers: April-May, white delicately veined with lilac, rarely tinged with purple.
Stem: A creeping rootstock covered by fleshy leaf bases.
Leaves: Trifoliate, on long stalks, bright yellowish-green, with scattered hairs.
Fruit: Capsules containing small seeds.

Wood-sorrel

Touch-me-not Balsam

Touch-me-not Balsam up to 1 m (3 ft)
Impatiens noli-tangere

Touch-me-not or Yellow Balsam (family *Balsaminaceae*) is an annual, with conspicuous yellow flowers from July to September. It grows up to 1 m (3 ft) in shady woods. Its leaves are large and broad, with serrated margins. The valves of its fruit capsules roll up when touched, scattering seeds.

Bloody Crane's-bill

GERANIUM FAMILY

Geranium sanguineum 10-40 cm (4-16 in)

Geraniaceae

The Bloody Crane's-bill is more than a handsome wild flower; it is a reminder that the bird known as a crane used to be native to Britain even if it has now become extinct here. How else could those who first named the plant have compared its beaked fruits with the bill of the bird unless it was a familiar sight! The plant itself is a fairly bushy perennial with striking purple-crimson flowers, rarely pink. Otherwise its general form is that of other members of the Geranium family. The fruits are formed of fused carpels, the long beak being formed by the fused styles. When ripe its fruits as they dry split out into elastically coiled sections which carry the single-seeded carpels upwards and outwards, scattering the seeds.

Habitat: Dry soils, especially on lime, woods, hedges, hills.
Flowers: June-September, usually solitary, bright crimson to purple, five sepals, five petals, ten stamens, three to five carpels.
Stem: Erect or spreading, hairy.
Leaves: Divided into 5-7 narrow lobes each divided into a further three lobes.
Fruit: Carpels fused, ending in a beak.

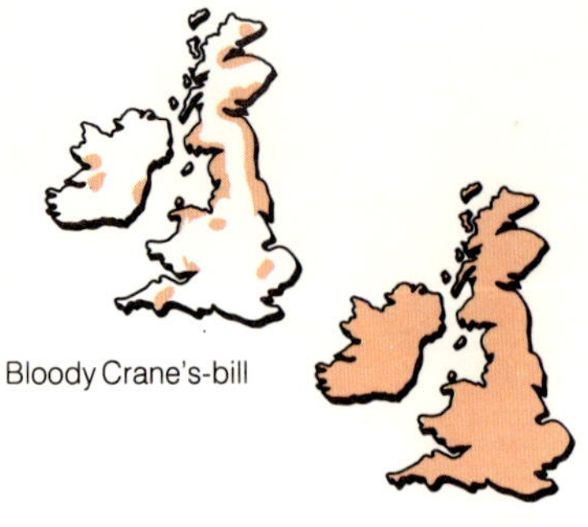

Bloody Crane's-bill

Herb-Robert

Herb-Robert 10-50 cm (4-20 in)
Geranium robertianum

Herb-Robert, named in honour of a French Cistercian monk, Abbot Robert, is a smaller annual version of the Crane's-bill whose foliage turns crimson in autumn. It is most remarkable for the multiplicity of its names: Poor Robin, Jenny Wren, Dragon's Blood, Dog's Toe, to name but a few.

Wood Spurge

SPURGE FAMILY

Euphorbia amygdaloides 30-80 cm (12-32 in)

Euphorbiaceae

The stems of spurges, when broken, exude a milky juice which in the past was used medicinally as a purgative. The scientific name of this perennial is taken from Euphorbus, physician to King Juba of ancient Mauretania in north-west Africa, who specialized in purgatives. The juice is also said to cure warts. Spurges can be recognized by their peculiar inflorescence: each flower is bell-shaped and inside is a single female flower surrounded by a dozen or more male flowers each consisting of one stamen. The female flower is composed of a single three-lobed ovary having three styles, each of which is cleft into two branches at its tip.

Habitat: Woods, scrubland.
Flowers: April-June, yellow.
Stem: Erect, unbranched, often tinged with red.
Leaves: Lanceolate, simple, margins smooth, undersides hairy.
Fruit: Rounded, stalked.

Wood Spurge

Purple Spurge

Purple Spurge 15-30 cm (6-12 in)
Euphorbia peplis

The Purple or Petty Spurge is unusual among spurges in that it grows flat to the ground, with several branches coming off at right angles to the root. It is an annual with small purple flowerheads, and is found on the sandy shores of South Wales and southern England, flowering during August and September.

Common Mallow

Malva sylvestris 45-120 cm (18-48 in)

MALLOW FAMILY
Malvaceae

Other name: Rags and Tatters

The Common Mallow is annual to perennial. It bears some resemblance to the familiar garden hollyhock, but there are many differences. The Mallow tends to sprawl and is more of a bush; a striking plant in its prime but after the flowers have died off it becomes ragged, and snails eat the leaves to tatters. Its method of pollination is of interest. The stamens are numerous and their stalks are united to form a tube. The 10-14 carpels, each with a style, form a ring within the shelter of the stamens. Cross-fertilization is ensured by the stamens ripening first and, after shedding their pollen on visiting insects, bending outwards and downwards. The styles now lengthen so that the stigmas are in the position originally occupied by the anthers, ready for other pollen-laden insects from other mallows. This plant has been used medicinally, for poulticing and for treating inflammation.

Habitat: Waysides, waste ground, hedgerows.
Flowers: June-October, in clusters, on short stalks, pale to dark pink with darker radiating lines, five petals slightly cleft, five sepals.
Stem: Erect, often sprawling, hairy.
Leaves: Often with small dark spot, divided into five toothed lobes.
Fruit: 10-14 segments united in a ring.

Common Mallow

Perennial Flax

Perennial Flax 30-60 cm (1-2 ft)
Linum anglicum

The Perennial Flax grows in dry, especially chalky grasslands. A delicately built plant of the family *Linaceae*, its slender stems are clothed in simple needle-shaped leaves arranged alternately and the whole topped with a spray of pale to bright blue flowers. The leaves appear to have only one central vein but often there are two others.

Common Dog-violet

VIOLET FAMILY
Violaceae

Viola riviniana 2.5-20 cm (1-8 in)

Other name: Dog Violet

'Dog' in the names of plants denotes something worthless or inferior as in Dog Rose, Dog Daisy and Dog's Parsley, Dog-violet being so called because it lacks scent. The flower of the Dog-violet is typical of the family, which also includes pansies. There are two upper petals and three lower ones, the lowest of the three being spurred. It is a low-growing perennial, almost hairless, with a rosette of leaves and the flowers borne on short lateral branches. With the Sweet Violet, particularly the cultivated forms, it has been used in salads, for making jellies, violet vinegar and crystallized violets. The Common Dog-violet, like the Sweet Violet, sometimes bears what are called cleistogamic flowers, that is small inconspicuous flowers permanently closed, which are self-fertilized. These occur in addition to the normal flowers.

Habitat: Grassy places, in open spaces or in woods, hedgerows, on high ground and on mountains.
Flowers: April-May, also sometimes July-September, blue-violet, unscented, five small sepals, five petals of differing shapes.
Stem: A rootstock.
Leaves: In a tuft, heart-shaped, on long stems, with small stipules.
Fruit: Oval capsules containing many small seeds.

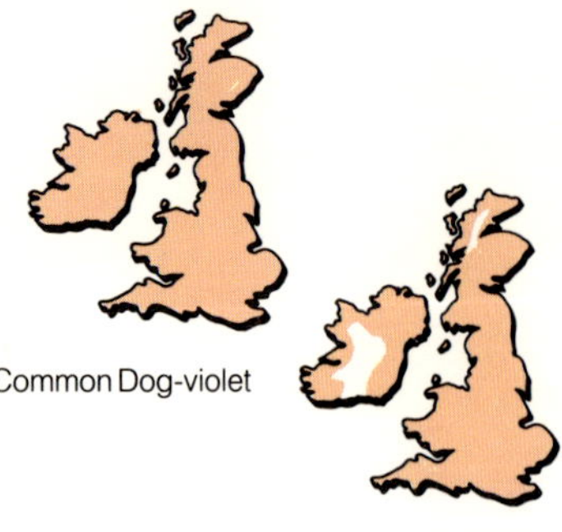

Common Dog-violet

Wild Pansy

Wild Pansy 10-30 cm (4-12 in)
Viola tricolor

The Wild Pansy or Heartsease, which may be annual or biennial, blooms from May to September in cornfields, on cultivated ground and in pastures as well as on waste ground. Its two upper petals are purple, the other three yellowish with conspicuous dark veins or honey-guides to direct insects.

Perforate St John's-wort

ST JOHN'S-WORT FAMILY

Hypericum perforatum 20-90 cm (8-36 in)

Hypericaceae

Other names: Common St John's Wort, Perforated St John's Wort

The Perforate St John's-wort is an erect perennial whose golden flowers are a common and attractive sight in many different places. The plant is called after St John the Baptist whose name is associated with Midsummer Day, June 24, when the flowers are at their peak. When the leaves are held up to the light the translucent oil glands in them look like pale green pinpricks, which accounts for the adjective 'perforate'. These glands give the plant its pungent smell. St John's-wort was formerly used to treat wounds and indeed has been called Balm of War and Balm of Warrior's Wounds. There is, however, some doubt whether these names arose from a belief in the healing powers of the plant. An alternative explanation is that the leaves have the appearance of being pierced in many places.

Habitat: Dry fields, open woods, grassy banks, thickets.
Flowers: May-August, golden yellow, star-shaped, in branched clusters, with minute black dots on petals and sepals.
Stem: Erect, hairless, marked with two longitudinal raised lines.
Leaves: Oval to linear, hairless, stalkless, in opposite pairs, with numerous, translucent, glandular dots.
Fruit: Long, pointed, multi-chambered, golden-brown capsules.

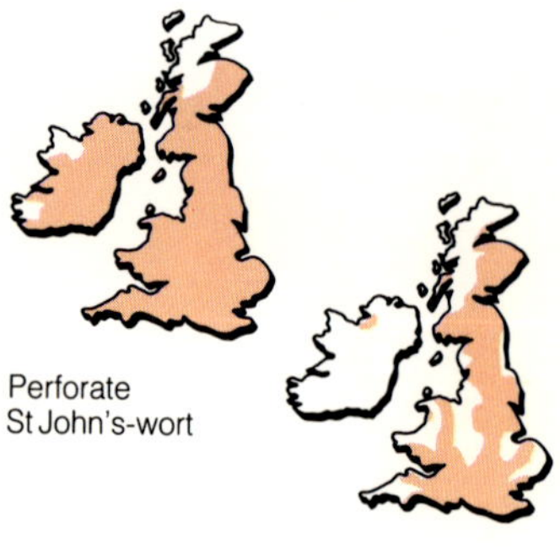

Perforate St John's-wort

Common Rock-rose

Common Rock-rose
Helianthemum chamaecistus
5-30 cm (2-12 in)

The perennial Common Rock-rose (family *Cistaceae*) is found on chalky downs, mainly in southern England. Its dainty flowers with five heart-shaped petals, with innumerable yellow stamens at the centre, are usually yellow but can be white, pink, orange or cream. Its stems trail along the ground.

Purple-loosestrife

LOOSESTRIFE FAMILY

Lythrum salicaria 50-200 cm (20-80 in)

Lythraceae

Other name: Willowstrife

The handsome Purple-loosestrife is a tall perennial growing from underground stems, with willow-like leaves and striking purple blossoms 2.5 cm (1 in) in diameter. Botanically, its main interest is in its elaborate mechanism for ensuring cross-pollination. The plant has three kinds of flowers. The 12 stamens are half short, half long. The style may be short, long or intermediate. In the first of the three forms the stigma is below all the anthers. In the second it is above them all. In the intermediate the stigma lies between the anthers of the two lengths of stamen. Long-styled flowers are fertilized by pollen from short- and intermediate-styled flowers; short-styled flowers are pollinated by long- and intermediate-styled flowers; and intermediate-styled flowers are pollinated by short- and long-styled flowers.

Habitat: By lakes, streams and ponds, and in marshes.
Flowers: June-September, purple, with six petals, flowers in whorled spikes.
Stem: Erect, tall, downy with four raised longitudinal lines.
Leaves: Sessile, lanceolate, simple, opposite or in whorls of three.
Fruit: A six-celled capsule.

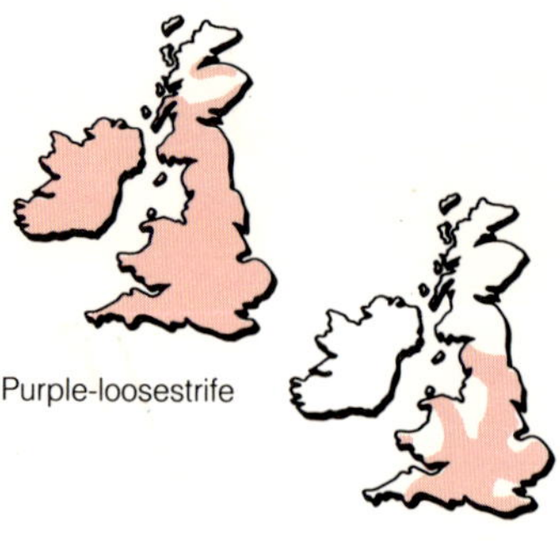

Purple-loosestrife

Spurge-laurel

Spurge-laurel 40-100 cm
Daphne laureola (16-39 in)

Spurge-laurel, of the family *Thymelaeaceae*, is an evergreen with stems up to 1 m (3 ft) tall bearing laurel-like leaves. It flowers from January to April, and the green flowers hang in bunches. There is a tubular calyx, with eight stamens but no petals. The fruit is a poisonous black berry.

Rosebay Willowherb

Epilobium angustifolium 20-120 cm (8-48 in)

WILLOWHERB FAMILY
Onagraceae

Other names: Rosebay, Flowering-willow, Fireweed

It is hard to believe that the Rosebay Willowherb, one of the largest and tallest of our perennial herbaceous plants, was fairly scarce in the early years of this century. It first attracted public notice during World War 2 when it began to spread over bombed sites in London and elsewhere. It grew on the ruins of buildings, on stony ledges and even on roofs, and soon became known as the Fireweed. The name is apt since one finds the plant in profusion where fire has destroyed a wood, or where trees have been cut down and burned and the ground is covered in wood ash. One reason for this dramatic proliferation and spread lies in its seed-dispersal. A single plant can produce 20,000 seeds and, when the capsules are ripe and have split, the slightest breath of wind carries the seeds, with their hairy parachutes, for long distances.

Habitat: Clearings in woods, on screes, in thickets.
Flowers: June-September, numerous in long, leafless terminal spikes, four sepals forming a dark purple calyx, four petals of unequal size, eight stamens, four-lobed stigma.
Stem: Erect, unbranched.
Leaves: Narrow, spirally arranged on stem, lanceolate, net-veined underneath, margins wavy.
Fruit: Long narrow capsules which split into four releasing seeds with long plumes of hairs.

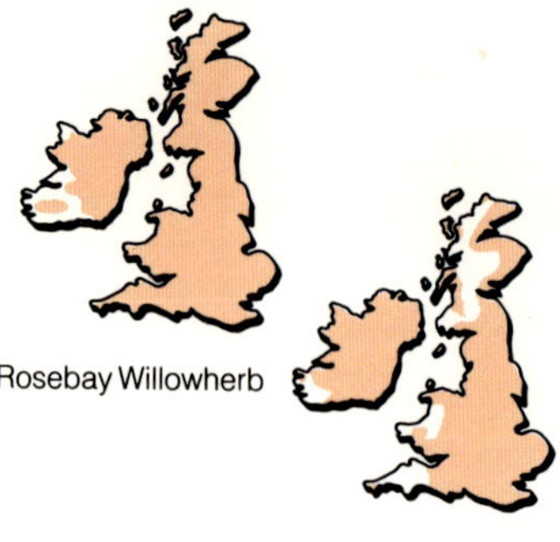

Mare's-tail 25-150 cm (10-60 in)
Hippuris vulgaris

From the family *Hippuridaceae,* the Mare's-tail is a perennial that grows underwater, its long stems bearing whorls of finely cut leaves, so that it looks like the Horsetail with which it has been confused. In June and July it throws up stalks above water which bear flowers with no petals and only one stamen and one carpel each.

Sanicle

Sanicula europaea 20-60 cm (8-24 in)

UMBELLIFER FAMILY
Umbelliferae

Other name: Wood Sanicle

There is only one place to look for Sanicle and that is in a wood. There are few plants so choosey as to where they grow. It is easily recognizable from its leaves which are glossy and deeply cut into three to five serrated lobes all arising from a perennial rootstock. There are few leaves on the stem and these are very small and are usually at the base of a flower stalk. The Sanicle was valued for its medicinal properties, and particularly for healing wounds, and its name comes from the Latin, *sanare*, to cure. It is said to be most efficacious when gathered on a dry day soon after the sun has dried away any dew. Its more modern use in herbalism is for cleansing the blood.

Habitat: Woods.
Flowers: May-July, dull white, in irregular globular groups.
Stem: Erect, unbranched.
Leaves: Glossy, rounded, deeply lobed, lobes serrated at margins.
Fruit: Rounded with hooked spines.

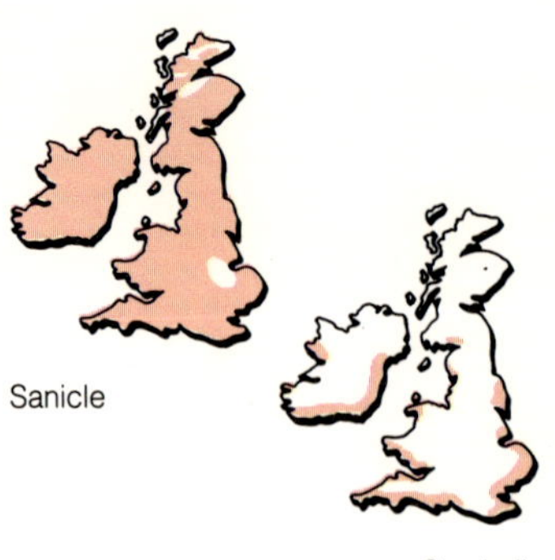

Sanicle

Sea-holly

Sea-holly 30-60 cm (1-2 ft)
Eryngium maritimum

The Sea-holly or Sea Eryngo is a perennial with holly-like leaves found on sandy or shingly beaches. It is nearly related to the delicate Sanicle but has a stiff texture. Like the Sanicle it was used medicinally and its roots were eaten as a vegetable. It has globular heads of bluish flowers.

Cow Parsley

UMBELLIFER FAMILY

Anthriscus sylvestris 60-90 cm (2-3 ft)

Umbelliferae

Other names: Wild Beaked Parsley, Bur Chervil

The Cow Parsley is an early spring flower and one of the most common of this family. A biennial, it can be distinguished when in bud by the way the flowers droop and later by its beaked fruits. Cow Parsley seems almost to epitomize the coming of summer. It pushes up its stems rapidly, once they start to grow, and blooms almost overnight it seems, to grace our roadside verges with the delicate lacery of its white flowers. Its beauty is unfortunately all too short-lived today when verges are kept clipped short. Its fruits, as is characteristic of the family *Umbelliferae*, split into two halves when ripe, each hanging from a central stalk. They are narrow, smooth and shiny and, unlike so many related species, are not ribbed nor do they contain canals filled with aromatic oils, as so many members of the family do.

Habitat: Shady places and hedgebanks.
Flowers: April-June, white umbels with 4-15 short rays.
Stem: Hollow upright, slightly grooved, hairy in lower part.
Leaves: Two to three times pinnate.
Fruit: Black or brown, smooth or bristly, beaked.

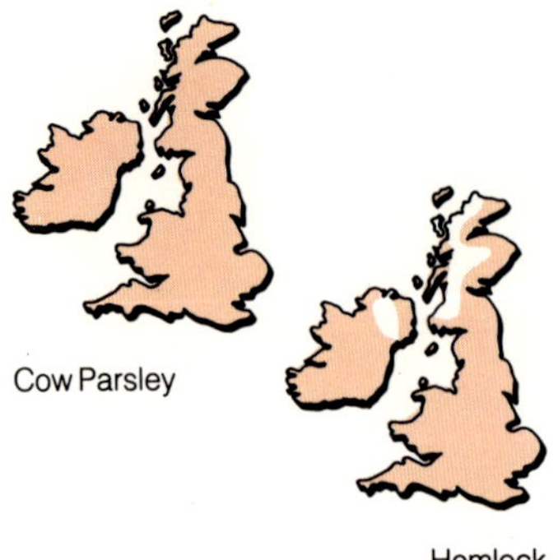

Hemlock up to 250 cm (8 ft)
Conium maculatum

Hemlock is a tall biennial growing up to 2.5 m (8 ft) high in hedgerows and on waste ground. It is a larger, coarser version of the Cow Parsley distinguished by its furrowed stems spotted with purple. It is a very poisonous plant widely used since classical times! The seeds are particularly poisonous.

Upright Hedge-parsley

Torilis japonica 60-90 cm (2-3ft)

UMBELLIFER FAMILY
Umbelliferae

The Upright Hedge-parsley is a perennial with stiff stems and multiple pinnate leaves. The flowers are white to pink and typical of this family, consisting of five petals, five stamens, a reduced calyx and an inferior ovary. Many species contain the word 'parsley' in their names: Cow Parsley, Hedge Parsley and Fool's Parsley are but three. The cultivated parsley did not reach England until 1548 and soon the name was being applied to one wild flower after another, all superficially very much alike. The Upright Hedge-parsley comes into bloom as the flowers of the Cow Parsley die off which is one way of identifying them.

Habitat: Woods, hedges, shady places.
Flowers: July-September, umbels stalked, white or pink.
Stem: Solid, rough.
Leaves: Rough, with hairs pressed close to the surface, one to three times pinnate, segments oval to lanceolate, deeply lobed and toothed.
Fruit: Thickly covered with incurved bristles which are not hooked.

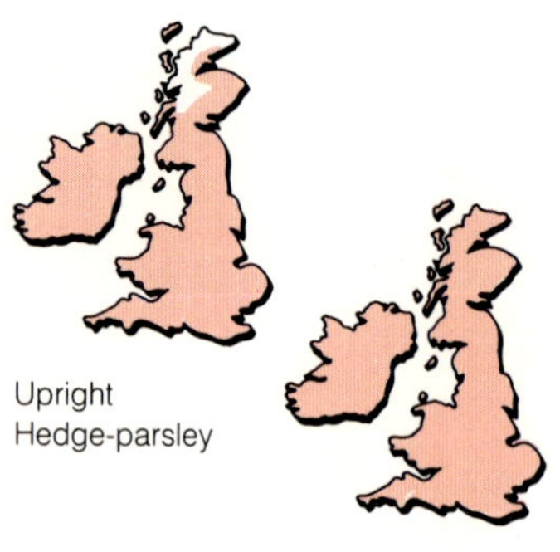

Hogweed 50-200 cm (20-80 in)
Heracleum sphondylium

Hogweed, also known as Common Cow Parsnip or Kecks, is a large, robust biennial growing in damp places. Its stem is deeply furrowed. Its umbels are composed of unusually large flowers. Those of the outer rim of each umbel are irregular, in that the petals facing outwards are much larger than those facing inwards.

Heather

Calluna vulgaris 30-60 cm (1-2 ft)

HEATH FAMILY
Ericaceae

Other name: Ling

Although Heather is usually a low perennial shrub it can at times reach a height of 1.2 m (4 ft). It is a plant found throughout the northern hemisphere, characteristically covering wide areas of acid soil rich in leaf litter or peat. Each flower in the leafy spikes includes four purple sepals below which are four greenish-purple bracts. Heather had and still has many uses: the flowers are rich in nectar from which a dark highly flavoured honey is obtained; brooms (besoms) are made from its stems; and it is used for thatching, fuel and on the island of Jura they make heather beer. The white-flowered variety has long been considered lucky.

Habitat: Heaths, moors, waysides, open woods, bogs and barren places generally.
Flowers: July-October, bell-shaped, pale purple, in leafy spikes. Four stamens, four fused carpels.
Stem: Woody, stiff, multi-branched.
Leaves: Small, simple, linear, overlapping each other in four longitudinal rows.
Fruit: Dry capsules to which the remains of the calyx and of the style continue to be attached.

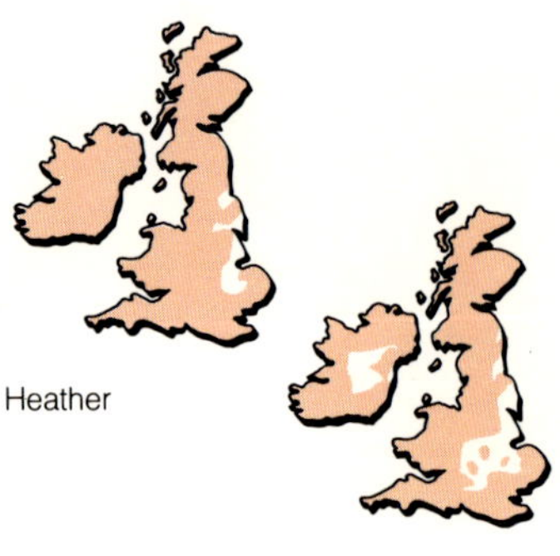

Bell Heather up to 60 cm (2 ft)
Erica cinerea

The habitat of the perennial Bell Heather, or Fine-leaved Heath, is similar to that of Heather but drier. The flowers are more obviously bell-shaped and reddish-purple, and the leaves are in whorls of threes, dark green, often with a touch of bronze.

Bilberry

HEATH FAMILY

Vaccinium myrtillus 20-60 cm (8-24 in)

Ericaceae

Other names: Whortleberry, Whinberry, Blaeberry, Bloom-berry

The Bilberry is a low-growing shrubby plant, a perennial with small toothed deciduous leaves. The pinkish flowers, which are borne in the axils of leaves, resemble those of Heather and the two are often found together. Each flower has four sepals that are joined forming a cup beneath which are four tiny bracts. The four petals form an almost spherical corolla with four teeth at the open end. Four stamens are present and four carpels form the ovary with a single long style. The young leaves have a beautiful rosy tint which turns later to dark green but they resume their rose colour again in autumn. The berries, known often as whorts, hurts or horts, are used in preserves and tarts, and also in wine-making. The leaves were formerly much used in medicine for dysentery, urinary troubles and for ulcers.

Habitat: Heaths, moors, open woods, except on limy soil.
Flowers: April-July, pink or greenish-pink, solitary or paired, globular, drooping.
Stem: Woody, angled, green.
Leaves: Oval, green, slightly toothed on margins.
Fruit: Edible black berries with a purplish bloom.

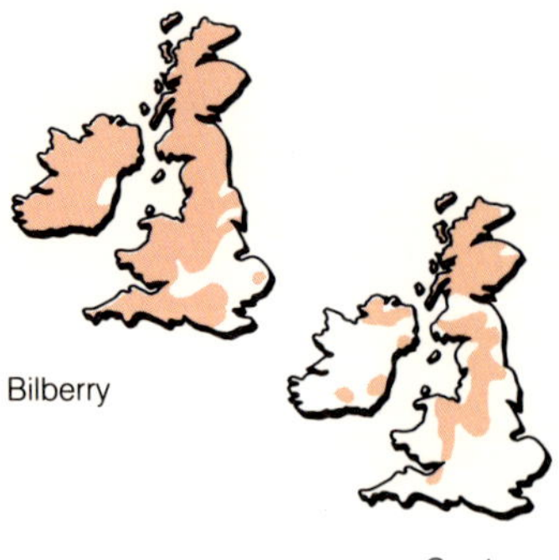

Cowberry up to 30 cm (1 ft)
Vaccinium vitis-idaea

Cowberry, or Red Whortleberry, is similar to the Bilberry but it is evergreen. It is often mistaken for the Cranberry, which it resembles except that the outer end of its leaves are broader. The berries are rich in Vitamin C and the leaves can be used as a tea.

Common Sea-lavender

SEA-LAVENDER FAMILY

Limonium vulgare 8-30 cm (3-12 in)

Plumbaginaceae

Other names: Marsh Rosemary, Wild Marsh Beet, Lavender Thrift, Ink Root

On muddy sea-flats or on sand dunes the Sea-lavender can often be seen covering extensive tracts with its pale purple blooms. It is a perennial with a woody, creeping rootstock from which arise clusters of basal leaves and angular stems that branch freely in the upper half, each branch bearing its quota of flowers. The whole plant has a withered look consistent with a habitat that is subject to persistent wind, an inhospitable soil and the corrosive effect of salt spray. Its flowers are similar in colour to those of the garden lavender, but have no scent. Sea-lavender has been used for centuries to make a gargle and as an astringent.

Habitat: Seashore and coastal salt marshes.
Flowers: July-August or later, lilac to lavender, in two-rowed, flat-topped clusters on branching stalks.
Stem: Rounded, smooth, leafless.
Leaves: Elliptical to broadly lanceolate, stalked, strongly pinnately veined.
Fruit: Dry seeds.

Common Sea-lavender

Thrift

Thrift 2-15 cm (¾-6 in)
Armeria maritima

The Thrift, or Sea Pink, grows on coastal cliffs and rocks and on high mountains. A perennial with grass-like leaves, it throws up slender stems each bearing clusters of rose-coloured flowers. Its tough rootstock goes surprisingly deep into the soil.

Primrose

Primula vulgaris 8-15 cm (3-6 in)

PRIMROSE FAMILY
Primulaceae

The Primrose, the *prima rosa*, is probably the most popular flower in the British flora, certainly in some parts of England. Fifty years ago it could have been described as particularly abundant, but then, as the countryside became more accessible with the advent of the family car, people came out from the towns and not only picked the blossoms but also dug up whole plants for their gardens. Today, especially near large towns, it is difficult to find Primroses blooming where formerly they carpeted the banks. It is a perennial and the flowers in each clump are on long stems all springing from one common, stout main stem which is so short as to be hidden among the bases of the leaves. Occasionally plants appear in which this main stem becomes much elongated, with the flowers on shorter stalks than usual carried at its top.

Habitat: Open woods, banks.
Flowers: March-May and sporadically in winter or late autumn, pale yellow, occasionally pink, with five cleft petals in a tube-like calyx of five green sepals.
Stem: A persistent rootstock.
Leaves: Wrinkled, tapering below to a stalk springing from the rootstock, underside a network of veins, hairy.
Fruit: Capsules opening at the top by five teeth.

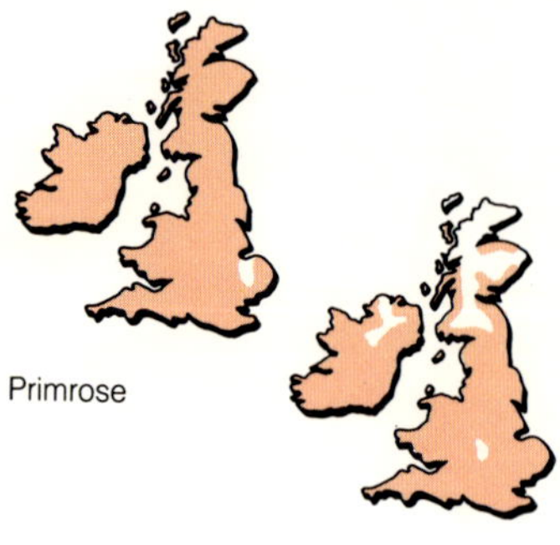

Primrose

Scarlet Pimpernel

Scarlet Pimpernel 6-30 cm
Anagallis arvensis (2½-12 in)

The Scarlet Pimpernel or Shepherd's Weather Glass is a small annual plant with tiny, delicate red five-petalled flowers growing on waste ground, among low herbage and in gardens. It closes its petals on the approach of rain, and the flowers do not open at all if there is no sun.

Common Centaury

GENTIAN FAMILY

Centaurium erythraea 2.5-30 cm (1-12 in)

Gentianaceae

The Common Centaury is an attractive annual with one particularly interesting feature: the tendency to twist certain parts of its flower. The flower consists of a five-lobed calyx containing a pink corolla in the form of a tube that is contracted at the top and then spreads into a five-lobed limb which, on casual glance, could be taken for five separate petals. Before the bud opens, however, the five lobes in this limb are twisted on each other. Twisting for a purpose is seen in the stamens and pistil. The stigma is mature when the bud opens and the anthers discharge their pollen in succession. Self-pollination is prevented, and cross-pollination ensured, by the style bending and carrying the stigma to one side while the stamens bend to the other. Later, stigma and anthers become erect and cross-pollination can then be effected.

Habitat: Dry grasslands.
Flowers: June-September, pink, with five petals, on very short stalks, in flat-topped clusters.
Stem: Erect, straight, ribbed, smooth, multi-branched from the base.
Leaves: Elliptical, mostly in a basal rosette, with a few narrower leaves in pairs up the stem, prominently three- to seven-veined.
Fruit: Capsules which split along the sides releasing numerous small seeds.

Common Centaury

Marsh Gentian

Marsh Gentian 10-40 cm (4-16 in)
Gentiana pneumonanthe

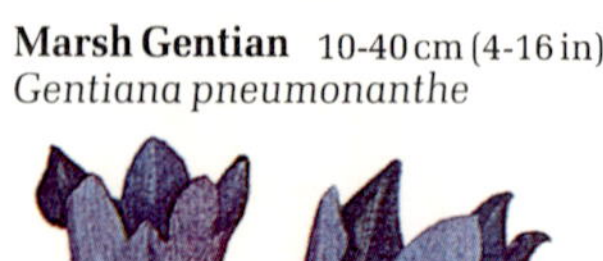

Marsh Gentian, or Calathian Violet, is also known as The Gift of Autumn, being a late-flowering (August to September) perennial found in bogs and marshes. The deep blue petals have green stripes on the outside of the tube they form. The specific name is a reminder that this plant was once used to treat lung diseases.

Bogbean

BOGBEAN FAMILY

Menyanthes trifoliata 10-30 cm (4-12 in)

Menyanthaceae

Other names: Buckbean, Marsh Trefoil, Beckbean

The Bogbean is one of the most beautiful plants in Britain both when seen close to and when it is viewed *en masse*. Each flower spike, arising from a perennial rootstock, bears three to twelve feathery blossoms each with a five-part calyx and a funnel-shaped corolla which is pure white tinged with pink. Bogbeans are seen at their best stretching across a bog or fringing a tarn with hundreds of flower spikes rising out of the water, their whiteness offset by the shining green of the leaves. The trefoil leaves bear a striking similarity to those of the seedling broad bean yet there is no relationship between them, the Bogbean being closely related to the gentians. The leaves when dried are aromatic and have been used in herbal tobacco. The dried leaves can also be used in a herbal tea, formerly used to treat scurvy.

Habitat: Shallow water in marshes, bogs and fens.
Flowers: April-June, pink and white in spikes, the petal tube expanding into five lobes fringed with long white hairs.
Stem: Short, smooth, hollow.
Leaves: Trefoil, bean-like, held well above the surface of the water.
Fruit: Capsule, rounded, bursting when ripe into two parts, containing few light brown, shiny seeds.

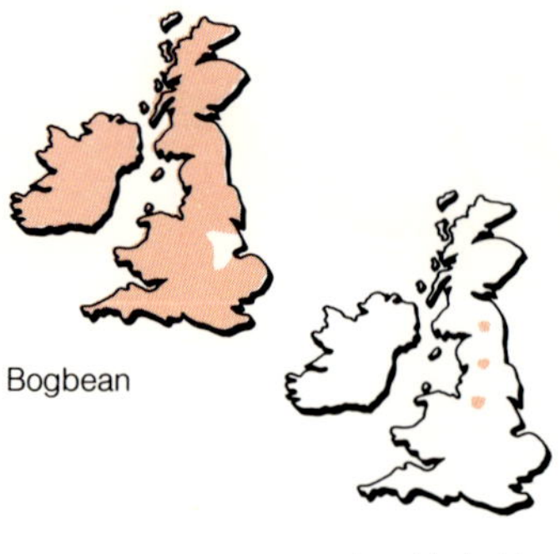

Bogbean

Jacob's-ladder

Jacob's-ladder 30-90 cm (1-3 ft)
Polemonium caeruleum

Jacob's-ladder, also known as Greek Valerian and Blue Jacob's-ladder, is a member of the Phlox *(Polemoniaceae)* family and owes its name to its long pinnate leaves. A herbaceous perennial, growing up to 90 cm (3 ft) and carrying terminal clusters of purplish-blue flowers. Found only in the Peak district.

Hedge Bindweed

BINDWEED FAMILY

Calystegia sepium up to 3 m (10 ft)

Convolvulaceae

Other names: Great Bindweed, Bellbine

Hedge Bindweed is a common perennial climbing plant the stems of which may ascend to 3 m (10 ft), climbing over shrubs and scrub or covering the ground in a writhing twisting mat. Its white underground stems, twisting and coiling, may go down an equal distance. It is when the plant climbs over heaps of dead scrub or wooden fences that the attractive blooms are shown at their best. That this plant has long attracted notice can be seen in the many common names by which it and its close relatives have been known: Withywind, Withwind, Woodbine, Ropebind and Hedge-bell. These reflect their persistent climbing habit and their tenacious hold on their supports, in which they are rivalled by the Honeysuckle. The two differ in that the latter twines clockwise whereas the Bindweeds twist anticlockwise.

Habitat: Woods, hedges, scrub, cultivated ground, waste land.
Flowers: June-September, large white bells, rarely pink, solitary.
Stem: Slender, climbing vine, smooth or nearly so.
Leaves: Heart- to arrow-shaped.
Fruit: Globose capsules.

Dodder 30-90 cm (1-3 ft) long
Cuscuta epithymum

In the same family as the Bindweed is the Dodder, an annual parasite on plants such as heather, gorse and clover. Its stems are slender reddish threads which attach themselves to the host plant by suckers, drawing nourishment from it. Its leaves are small scales; its flowers are in pink clusters.

Woodruff

Galium odoratum 30-60 cm (1-2 ft)

BEDSTRAW FAMILY
Rubiaceae

Other names: Sweet Woodruff, Herb Barnaby

Woodruff is a perennial which creeps by means of a thin rootstock and throws up slender stems. It is a change to find a plant which, instead of being named a harbinger of spring, has been chosen as the herald that winter is over. A 14th-century quotation has it: 'Away is their winter wo, when woderove springeth.' Its most remarkable feature is its sweet scent, from the flowers and also the leaves, most in evidence when the plant is dying off, when it smells of new-mown hay. Indeed, its Anglo-Saxon name is *wudurofe*, *rofe* meaning fragrant. At one time it was strewn on the floor, put in beds and placed among the linen, since it retains its perfume for a long time. It was also believed to deter clothes' moth.

Habitat: Woods and shady places.
Flowers: April-June, small, white, in leaf axils at the tops of shoots, each composed of four sepals, a funnel of four fused petals forming almost a bell, four stamens and two carpels.
Stem: Unbranched, almost hairless.
Leaves: Small, lanceolate, in whorls of six at the base of the stem, seven to nine near the top.
Fruit: Globular, covered with five hooked bristles.

Woodruff

Lady's Bedstraw

Lady's Bedstraw 15-100 cm
Galium verum (6-39 in)

Lady's Bedstraw is a perennial on dry banks and downs with a creeping rootstock sending out runners from which smooth square stems arise. The slender leaves are in whorls of eight to twelve. The plant is also called Yellow Bedstraw and is conspicuous by its small yellow flowers massed at the ends of the stems.

Common Comfrey

FORGET-ME-NOT FAMILY

Symphytum officinale 30-60 cm (1-2 ft) *Boraginaceae*

Other names: Blackwort, Boneset, Knitbone, Knitback, Ass Ear

The Common Comfrey is a stout, robust perennial long credited with medicinal properties. It can be cooked and eaten as a green vegetable but care should be taken because the leaves look something like those of the Foxglove, which are poisonous. A herbal tea can also be brewed from the leaves. The main virtue claimed for it, however, was that it helped to set broken bones and recent analysis has shown that it contains phosphorus. Its alleged value as a bone-setter is reflected in its common names and its healing properties in its scientific name, *symphyo* being Greek for heal or unite. In medieval Latin *officina* meant the storeroom of a monastery where medicines were kept.

Habitat: Banks of streams and rivers.
Flowers: May-July, purple, yellow or white, sometimes changing from one colour to another; each flower consists of a five-toothed calyx, five petals forming a funnel, five stamens and a four-segmented ovary.
Stem: Erect, much branched, softly hairy.
Leaves: Broadly lanceolate.
Fruit: Black, shiny, surrounded by the persistent calyx and containing four small nuts.

Lungwort 30-45 cm (12-18 in)
Pulmonaria officinalis

Lungwort was often used in the treatment of lung diseases. It is a perennial, 30-45 cm (12-18 in) high, with lanceolate leaves spotted with a paler green. Its pale purple flowers appear during June and July and are similar in structure to those of the Common Comfrey.

Field Forget-me-not

Myosotis arvensis 15-30 cm (6-12 in)

FORGET-ME-NOT FAMILY
Boraginaceae

Other names: Field Scorpion-grass, Common Scorpion-grass

Of the many romantic sounding names of plants that came into being in the 16th century, none is more familiar, easily remembered or touching in its sentiments than that of the Forget-me-not. The flower was supposed to ensure that those wearing it would never be forgotten by their lovers. This was in the early part of the century. Less than 50 years later the name 'scorpion grass' was coined seemingly in harsh contradiction, but 'scorpion' here refers merely to the form of the flower, which twists in a fancied resemblance to a scorpion's tail. The Field Forget-me-not may be annual or biennial, according to circumstances. It is the most common of several species carrying the generic name *Myosotis*. This is from the Greek and means 'mouse-ears', a reference to the shape of the leaves.

Habitat: Dry shady places.
Flowers: May-July, September-October, grey-blue, in coiled one-sided spikes, sepals form cup-shaped tube covered with hooked hairs, five petals forming a corolla with flat lobes.
Stem: Erect, slender, softly hairy.
Leaves: Basal leaves oval forming a rosette, stem leaves lanceolate.
Fruit: Dark brown, shiny achenes.

Field Forget-me-not

Viper's-bugloss

Viper's-bugloss up to 90 cm (3 ft)
Echium vulgare

Viper's-bugloss is a handsome biennial growing up to 90 cm (3 ft) tall with flowers suggestive of a viper's mouth with the tongue protruding. It has a short flowering season, June to July. The flowers are bright red-rose on first opening and change through purple to blue. The stems and leaves are covered with small prickly bristles.

Water Mint

MINT FAMILY

Mentha aquatica 30-120 cm (1-4 ft)

Labiatae

Other names: Hairy Mint, Capitate Mint

The Water Mint is the most common of our native mints often growing in extensive masses in wet places and distinguished by its stalked oval leaves, downy on both sides, velvety to the touch, and by its lilac flowers crowded into globular heads at the tops of the stems. Its scent is strong and not very pleasant. The flowering part of the stem often bears additional whorls of the lilac flowers clustering in the axils of the upper leaves. The Water Mint is a rank-growing perennial with a slender, creeping rootstock. It is one of several of our mints that have been cultivated for centuries as aromatic potherbs and as a source of aromatic essential oils. The best-known is the related peppermint from which menthol is obtained.

Habitat: Marshes, ditches, river banks, edges of streams.
Flowers: July-September, individual flowers tiny, lilac to pink, calyx tubular, acutely five-lobed, corolla of four petals with one notched at the apex, four anthers, ovary four-lobed.
Stem: Square in section, hairy, often purplish.
Leaves: Oval, pointed at apex, margins toothed.
Fruit: Four smooth achenes.

Gipsywort up to 90 cm (3 ft)
Lycopus europaeus

Gipsywort is a perennial with a creeping rootstock and erect, square stem up to 90 cm (3 ft) high that grows at edges of ponds, ditches and streams. Its leaves are long, elliptical, in opposite pairs, their margins deeply indented. The small flowers, white dotted with purple, are grouped in the axils of the leaves.

Selfheal

MINT FAMILY
Labiatae

Prunella vulgaris 8-30 cm (3-12 in)

Other names: Common Selfheal, Carpenter's Herb, Hook-heal, Sicklewort, Prunella, All Heal, Sloughheal

Several of our wild flowers have received this name, but this species is recognized by herbalists as the true Selfheal. It has been used, at least since the Middle Ages, for internal and external application, almost a universal panacea. A perennial with a creeping rootstock it throws up flowering branches bearing a terminal, cylindrical flower-head with two leaves standing out around the head like a sort of collar. The flowers forming each head do not all come out at once, which gives the head a ragged appearance. The flowers are of two kinds, large and small, the first being perfect, the second lacking anthers.

Habitat: Pastures and waysides.
Flowers: July-September, purplish-blue, in whorls of six, with small green bracts subtending each whorl; the upper lip of the corolla is erect, the lower lip spreads into three lobes.
Stem: Square, more or less hairy.
Leaves: Leaves oval, margins toothed or entire, somewhat hairy.
Fruit: Made up of four achenes.

Selfheal

Bugle

Bugle 10-30 cm (4-12 in)
Ajuga reptans

Bugle is a creeping perennial with erect stems, square in section, bearing whorls of deep purplish flowers in the axils of leaves. The leaves are in pairs, each pair at right angles to the adjacent pair. When the flowers open the style is already mature. The anthers do not shed their pollen until the ovary has been fertilized.

Hedge Woundwort

Stachys sylvatica 60-120 cm (2-4 ft)

MINT FAMILY
Labiatae

Other names: Hedge Stachys, Blind Nettle, Hedge Archangel, Cow's Weather Wind, Nettle Foot

Hedge Woundwort is a branched hairy perennial with a rootstock that sends out stems underground. It is noticeably hairy and has a strong unpleasant smell when crushed. As the name suggests, like the other woundworts, it had long been been used to treat wounds. The suffix 'wort' indicates a plant having medicinal properties or one used for food. The tuberous roots of the Hedge Woundwort are edible and are full of nutriment and the young shoots can be eaten like asparagus. The plant also yields a yellow dye. The name *Stachys* for this common and not very attractive plant is from the Greek for spike, a reference to the way the flowers are arranged in a terminal spike.

Habitat: Woods, hedges, in shade.
Flowers: June-September, in whorls of 6-10, calyx five-lobed, corolla reddish-purple, two-lipped, upper lip forming a hood over stamens, lower lip three-lobed.
Stem: Stout, quadrangular, densely covered with whitish stiff hairs.
Leaves: Resemble those of Common Nettle, opposite stalked, ovate with triangular apex, margins toothed, covered with long stiff hairs.
Fruit: Smooth achenes, rounded at the top.

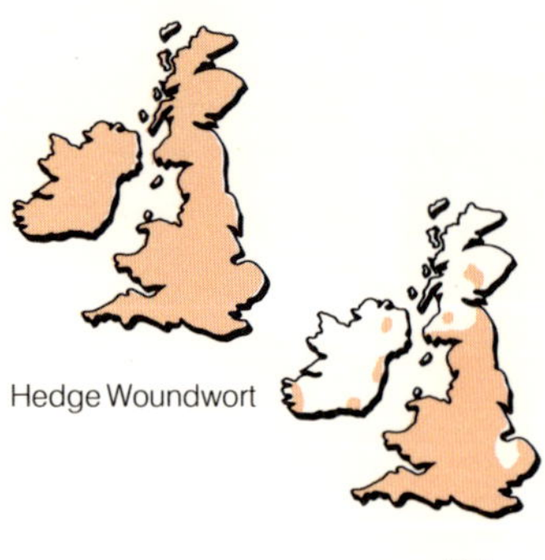

Betony 15-60 cm (6-24 in)
Betonica officinalis

A smaller and more graceful plant than the Hedge Woundwort, the Betony has flowers nearer purple in colour and grouped in denser spikes. This perennial has been highly prized for its healing virtues and its name is a corruption of *Vettonica*, after a Spanish tribe, the *Vettones*, who used it as a medicine.

Black Horehound

Ballota nigra 40-100 cm (16-39 in)

MINT FAMILY
Labiatae

Other name: Foetid Horehound

The Old English name for this plant was *hare hune*, meaning a hoary plant. It evolved over the centuries to horehound and has nothing to do with any canine breed. The use of the word 'black' is also misleading but arose in the first place to distinguish the plant from the White Horehound, belonging to another genus, which slightly resembles it in form but is white all over with down. The Black Horehound is a coarse, bushy but straggly perennial with leaves and flowers like a White Dead-nettle, except that the flowers are a showy reddish-purple. It has a very unpleasant smell. The odour of this plant is so strong and so offensive that once experienced it will always be recognized.

Habitat: Waysides, hedgebanks and waste ground.
Flowers: May-September, reddish-purple, numerous, in whorls in the axils of the upper leaves.
Stem: Erect, branching, hairy.
Leaves: Dark green, heart-shaped to oval, stalked, with toothed margins.
Fruit: Achenes.

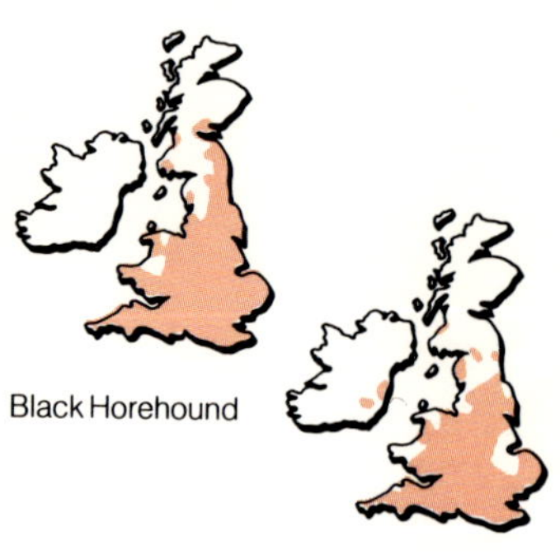

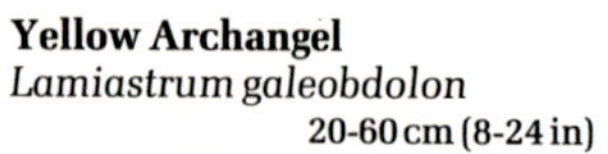

Yellow Archangel
Lamiastrum galeobdolon
20-60 cm (8-24 in)

The Yellow Archangel is a perennial that grows in woods and is similar to the White Dead-nettle. Other names are Yellow Dead-nettle and Weasel-snout. It is conspicuous because of its butter-yellow flowers the lower lip of which is streaked with reddish-brown. Like the Black Horehound it is strong smelling.

White Dead-nettle

Lamium album 20-60 cm (8-24 in)

MINT FAMILY
Labiatae

Other names: Blind Nettle, Deaf Nettle, Dumb Nettle, Dummy Nettle, Snake Flower

The White Dead-nettle, a perennial, is a favourite with bees because of its abundant nectar. This is reflected in two other common names: Bee Nettle and Suck Bottle. It is a useful plant by which to study the structure of a typical flower of the *Labiatae* family, that is, a flower suggestive of the open mouth of a snake. Indeed, another name is Snake Flower. The five sepals form a ten-ribbed tube with five teeth on the upper margin. The five petals form a tube spreading at the top into two parts. The upper of these forms a hood covering the stamens and styles. The lower part forms a platform on which insects seeking the nectar can alight.

Habitat: Waysides, waste places, hedgerows, especially where there is plenty of long grass.
Flowers: May-September but may be seen in bloom at all times of the year, white, in whorls of 6-12 in axils of upper leaves.
Stem: Erect, square in cross-section and with tough, persistent, underground stems.
Leaves: Roughly heart-shaped but pointed at the apex, in pairs alternating at right angles to each other.
Fruit: Composed of four small achenes, each containing one seed.

White Dead-nettle

Cat-mint

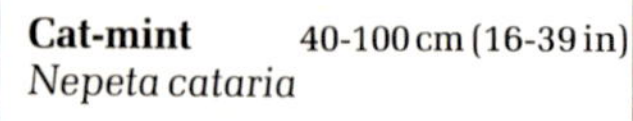

Cat-mint 40-100 cm (16-39 in)
Nepeta cataria

Cat-mint, a perennial, grows on open hedgebanks. It has heart-shaped leaves, with toothed margins. Its white flowers are in whorls in the axils of the leaves and many such whorls form the terminal spikes of flowers. It is named from the habit of domestic cats of rolling on it.

Wood Sage

Teucrium scorodonia 15-60 cm (6-24 in)

MINT FAMILY
Labiatae

Other names: Sage-leaved Wood Germander, Wood Germander

Wood Sage looks so like the garden sage, and is so common, especially in woods, that it is easy to recognize. It is an erect, shrubby perennial, which has long been used in infusions as a herbal tonic. The arrangement of the greenish-yellow flowers, as well as the flowers themselves, is unusual. The main stem ends in slender branches each of which bears flowers in loose spikes in pairs and all to one side. The individual flower consists of an unequally five-toothed calyx, subtended by a bract, within which the corolla of petals is deeply cleft in two, so that it does not form a hood over the stamens and the long style, the lower lip being three-lobed with the middle lobe much larger than the other two.

Habitat: Woods, hedgerows, scrub, heaths, not on lime.
Flowers: June-October, small, greenish-yellow, in one-sided leafless spikes.
Stem: Erect, square in section, hairy, with creeping underground stems.
Leaves: Heart-shaped, stalked, wrinkled, sage-like, pale grey undersurface.
Fruit: Groups of four achenes.

Wood Sage

Ground-ivy

Ground-ivy 15-45 cm (6-18 in)
Glechoma hederacea

Ground-ivy has little to do with the more familiar climbing creeper except that it is a perennial and creeps over the ground, as Ivy often does. It throws up flowering stems 15-45 cm (6-18 in) high. The purple flowers, in whorls of three in the axils of the leaves, can be seen from March to June.

Deadly Nightshade

NIGHTSHADE FAMILY

Atropa belladonna up to 1.5 m (5 ft)

Solanaceae

Other name: Dwale

A tall, stout perennial, with many branches and bearing black, very poisonous berries, Deadly Nightshade is well known by name but often confused with the Woody Nightshade or Bittersweet. 'Nightshade' is from the Anglo-Saxon *nihtscada*, meaning a narcotic. The alternative common name is medieval English from the Danish *dvale*, or trance. Although deadly poisonous the plant has been much used in medicine and as a cosmetic, especially by theatrical ladies (hence *belladonna*) for blanching the skin, removing freckles and dilating the pupils of the eyes. It has also been the source of a valuable sedative drug, atropine. It can be distinguished from other nightshades by its solitary flowers which are dull purplish-blue.

Habitat: Open woods and waste places, especially on limy soils.
Flowers: June-August, bell-shaped, solitary, purplish-blue, with a five-toothed calyx, five petals forming a tube, five stamens and two carpels with a long style, in axils of leaves.
Stem: Long, slender but tough, well-branched.
Leaves: Oval, ending in a point.
Fruit: Glossy black berries, sweet but very poisonous.

Bittersweet 30-200 cm (12-80 in)
Solanum dulcamara

Bittersweet, a climbing or prostrate perennial, also known as Woody Nightshade, has oval-pointed leaves, often with two leaflets at the base. Its bright purple flowers have a yellow cone at the centre, formed by the anthers. Its sprays of berries are first green (and sweet), then yellow and finally red (and bitter).

Great Mullein

FIGWORT FAMILY

Verbascum thapsus 30-200 cm (1-6½ ft)

Scrophulariaceae

Other names: Aaron's Rod, Adam's Blanket, Adam's Flannel

The Great Mullein is a bulky biennial the height of a man, carrying stiff spikes of yellow flowers. Its bulk is made up of woolly lanceolate leaves densely crowded at the base of the plant but becoming smaller up the stem until they are no more than small bracts. The lowest flowers open first. The lasting impression conveyed by Great Mullein is of a plant encased closely in cottonwool, due to its coating of multi-rayed, star-shaped hairs. Three of the five stamens are also hairy. The large leaves were formerly used as wicks and poultices and the plant has long been famous in herbal medicine. The Romans extracted a yellow dye from the petals.

Habitat: Waysides, waste ground, coppices, especially on dry and chalky soils.
Flowers: June-August, yellow, made up of five woolly, united sepals, five petals forming a tube then opening out into free lobes, five stamens and a two-chambered ovary.
Stem: Stout, erect, woolly.
Leaves: Lanceolate, large, grey, flannel-like, their bases continued as wings down the stem to the next leaf base.
Fruit: Capsules opening into two valves.

Great Mullein

Common Toadflax

Common Toadflax up to 60 cm (2 ft)
Linaria vulgaris

The Common Toadflax, or Yellow Toadflax, is an erect, herbaceous perennial up to 60 cm (2 ft) high with numerous grass-like greyish-green leaves and dense spikes of yellow snapdragon-like flowers each with a long spur at the base. The name reflects the flax-like appearance of the leaves.

Foxglove

Digitalis purpurea 1.2 m (4 ft)

FIGWORT FAMILY
Scrophulariaceae

Other names: Dead Man's Bells, Purple Foxglove

A tall perennial, shallow-rooted, with a mass of leaves at the base from which the flowering stems arise, the Foxglove gives plenty of colour in favoured places in summer. Its flowers, beautifully spotted inside the bell, are arranged in a one-sided manner on the stem due to a curious twisting of each flower stalk. There is some doubt about the origin of its picturesque name but all agree it has nothing to do with the woodland animal, although the fox's scent sometimes hangs heavy on the air where the plant is growing. One explanation is that the name comes from the Anglo-Saxon *foxes glofe*. Another is that it means folk's-glove or fairy glove. The leaves of the plant have been an important source of the drug digitalin, used to slow down the heart-beat.

Habitat: Waste land, woods, dry slopes, not on limy soils.
Flowers: June-July, purple, calyx of five unequal sepals joined in a tube, petals forming a bell with four or five lobes on the rim, two long and two short stamens, ovary two-chambered.
Stem: Erect, unbranched, downy.
Leaves: Lanceolate, slightly downy with toothed margins, wrinkled.
Fruit: Capsules with numerous fine seeds.

Foxglove

Common Figwort

Common Figwort 100-120 cm (3-4 ft)
Scrophularia nodosa

The Common Figwort, or Knotted Figwort, is a tall herbaceous perennial, 100-120 cm (3-4 ft) high with a strong unpleasant smell growing in damp bushy places in woods and elsewhere in shade. Its leaves are smooth, heart-shaped tapering to a point. Its flowers, a dingy purple, appear during June to September.

Germander Speedwell

Veronica chamaedrys 20-40 cm (8-16 in)

FIGWORT FAMILY
Scrophulariaceae

Other names: Bird's Eye, Forget-me-not (not to be confused with the well-known flower of that name)

The outstanding feature of the Germander Speedwell is the bright blue of its flowers, which makes them very conspicuous even though they are tiny. Indeed, few plants can be more rewarding for their examination with a magnifying glass than this common and abundant, sprawling perennial found in such a variety of habitats. The bright blue of the flowers tends to fade to pink with blue lines. The stamens are blue; even the style is blue. Another feature best revealed under a glass, and one which marks this species from all other speedwells, is the line of hairs on each side of the stem which move around at each pair of leaves. 'Speedwell' is believed to indicate how readily the petals drop after fertilization. 'Germander' is a corruption of two Greek words meaning 'ground-oak', from a fancied resemblance of its leaves to those of the oak.

Habitat: Woods, pastures, waysides, hedgerows.
Flowers: April-June, bright blue with conspicuous white 'eye' at the centre, four sepals, four unequal petals, two stamens, one style.
Stem: Sprawling, slender with opposite lines of hairs, throwing up erect flowering stems.
Leaves: Oval, pointed, hairy, stalkless or nearly so, opposite, margins coarsely toothed.
Fruit: Two-celled, flattened, heart-shaped capsules.

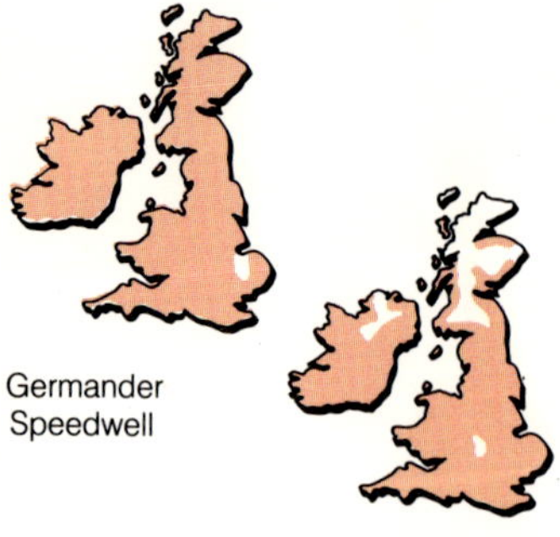

Common Field-speedwell
Veronica persica
10-40 cm (4-16 in)

The Common Field-speedwell or Buxbaum's Speedwell is a sprawling annual that could be confused with the Germander Speedwell. It is a native of western Asia that has become widely naturalized throughout Europe, including Britain. Its flowers are solitary, not in spikes.

Marsh Lousewort

Pedicularis palustris 15-45 cm (6-18 in)

FIGWORT FAMILY
Scrophulariaceae

Other names: Lousewort, Red Rattle, Marsh Red-rattle

As its name suggests, the Marsh Lousewort is parasitic on the roots of marsh plants and grasses generally. It is a striking biennial with almost fern-like leaves and reddish-pink flowers, its stems often purplish, its leaves at times tinged with the same colour. The flowers are an unusual shape. The petals are fused in their lower part, forming a tube which is wide at the mouth where it divides into two. One half forms a tube hiding the stamens; the other half forms three lobes that fold back. This lower half forms a landing stage for insects visiting the flower for nectar. They pull the anthers on to their backs, so carrying away the pollen. The plant itself has been much in demand in the past for the external treatment of wounds and, boiled in port wine, to assist in their healing.

Habitat: Marshes, bogs, damp fields.
Flowers: May-September, reddish-pink to rosy purple, calyx often reddish, with two leafy lobes.
Stem: Single, multi-branched, nearly hairless.
Leaves: Pinnate, deeply cut producing six pairs of leaflets and one leaflet at the apex, each leaflet being toothed along the margins.
Fruit: Capsules with small seeds, enclosed in a bladder-like calyx.

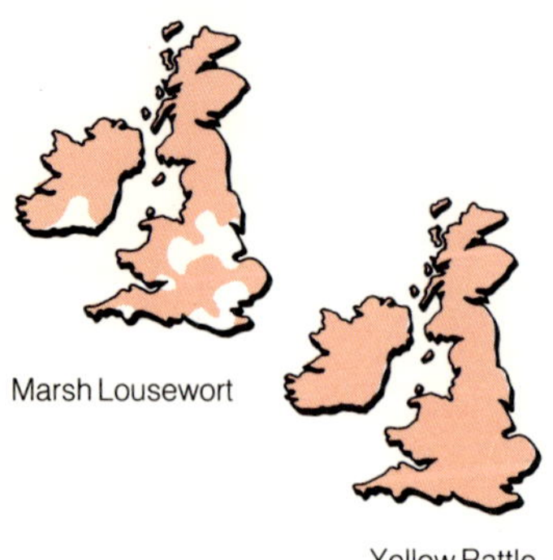

Yellow Rattle 12-40 cm (5-16 in)
Rhinanthus minor

Yellow Rattle, also known as Cock's-comb, is an annual associated with cornfields and is closely related to the Red Rattle but looks unlike it in general form. Its flowers are pinkish yellow and its leaves are lanceolate. It also is semi-parasitic on the roots of other plants and, as in the Red Rattle, the seeds rattle in its bladder-like calyx.

Common Butterwort

Pinguicula vulgaris 5-15 cm (2-6 in)

BUTTERWORT FAMILY
Lentibulariaceae

This singular and beautiful perennial can be readily missed by the unobservant or taken to be a kind of violet. It is insectivorous. The upper surface of the leaves is covered with glandular hairs and has an oily appearance (Latin *pinguis* means oily) as though it is coated with butter. An insect alighting is trapped as if on a flypaper. The leaf then curls inwards completely trapping it. The glandular hairs secrete digestive juices which dissolve the proteins in the insect's body and these are absorbed by the leaf, after which the leaf opens out again. Any indigestible remains are washed away by rain or dislodged by the wind and the leaf is ready to trap its next victim. Taken raw the plant causes vomiting and is a purgative. It is, however, used in Lapland to curdle milk.

Habitat: Wet, boggy land, mainly on hills and mountains.
Flowers: May-July, on long slender stalks, violet, spurred, calyx forms five unequal lobes, corolla two-lipped, upper lip bilobed, lower trilobed.
Stem: Erect, two or three to each plant, drooping at the top.
Leaves: Thick, oval, stalkless, forming a rosette, upper surface pale green, undersurface almost white, edges curling upwards.
Fruit: Capsules with many small seeds.

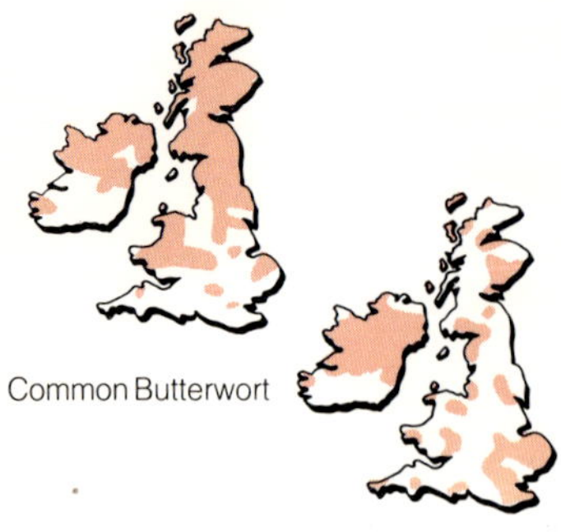

Greater Bladderwort 15-45 cm
Utricularia vulgaris (6-18 in)

The Greater or Common Bladderwort, also perennial, is a more specialized insect-eater. It is aquatic, wholly submerged, its leaves finely divided. At intervals are bladders, each with a valve bearing sensitive hairs. Any animal up to a tadpole touching these is sucked in and digested.

Greater Plantain

Plantago major 12-23 cm (5-9 in)

PLANTAIN FAMILY
Plantaginaceae

Other names: Great Plantain, Lamb's Tongue Plantain, Waybread, White Man's Foot (USA)

The Greater Plantain, a perennial, is one of the few despised wild flowers, for it lacks beauty and is a pest on cultivated ground and in lawns. However, it does have one use: its seed-heads are used to feed seed-eating cage birds. The most noticeable features of the flower are the purple stamens. When the plant is growing among tall grass the leaves adopt an erect posture. Elsewhere, and especially on well-trodden paths, the broad leaves, strongly ribbed on the underside, and springing direct from the roots, lie on the surface of the ground. The flowers are normally wind-pollinated although some pollination by insects does occur.

Habitat: Waste ground, paths, lawns, cultivated ground.
Flowers: June-August or later, greenish-yellow or pale brown, crowded along the upper half of the stalk, each flower consisting of four persistent sepals, a four-lobed corolla, four stamens and a single style.
Stem: Stem lacking; flower stalks erect, downy or hairless, ribbed.
Leaves: Broadly oval, forming a rosette.
Fruit: Capsules which split transversely.

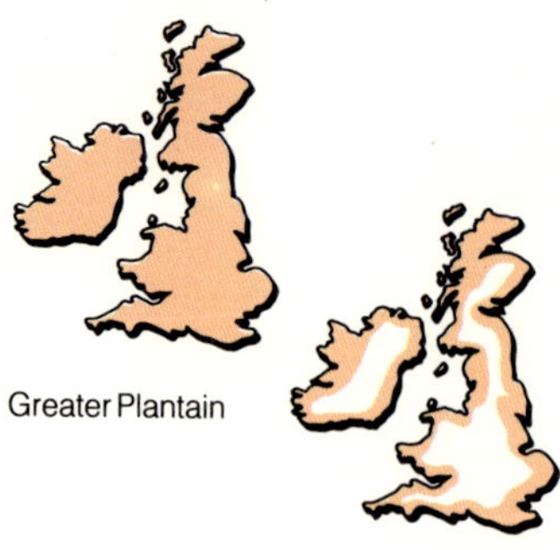

Sea Plantain 3-30 cm (1-12 in)
Plantago maritima

The Sea Plantain grows in salt marshes near the coast and also on mountains. It is a small version of the familiar plantains with almost grass-like leaves with three to five veins, sometimes slightly toothed on the margins. It is a perennial and its tiny flowers, on long spikes, are brownish-pink.

Honeysuckle

Lonicera periclymenum up to 6 m (20 ft)

HONEYSUCKLE FAMILY
Caprifoliaceae

Other name: Woodbine

'And woodbine scents the way' according to the folksong. Although the name 'woodbine' is also applied to bindweeds there can be little doubt that this quotation refers to the Honeysuckle. When this climbing perennial was more common it was the practice to pick sprigs of it in summer and take them indoors so that the fragrance of the Honeysuckle became inseparable from the country cottage. The scent is strongest at night and attracts night-flying moths whose long tongues can reach down into the corolla tube to drink the nectar which may half-fill the tube. The vine twines so strongly around its support that, if this is a sapling, it leaves a spiral groove in the bark, impeding the growth of the tree. The berries are poisonous.

Habitat: Copses and hedgerows or among scrub.
Flowers: June-October, yellow tinged with red, in clusters, calyx five-toothed, corolla tubular, 5 cm (2 in) long, ending in two lips.
Stem: A tough climbing vine twining clockwise.
Leaves: Oval with a slight point, stalked in the lower part of the vine, others stalkless, opposite.
Fruit: Clusters of six to twelve round red berries.

Moschatel 5-10 cm (2-4 in)
Adoxa moschatellina

Moschatel, of the family *Adoxaceae*, is a low-growing perennial of damp shady places with leaves twice trefoil that has two most attractive alternative names, Townhall Clock and Five-faced Bishop. Each stalk bears at its top five greenish-yellow flowers. One lies horizontally at the summit; the other four are arranged like clock faces.

Common Valerian

VALERIAN FAMILY
Valerianaceae

Valeriana officinalis 90-120 cm (3-4 ft)

Other names: All-heal, Cat Valerian

Common Valerian grows from an underground stem or rootstock from which stolons are given out, indicating it is a perennial. It has a bitter taste and an aromatic smell, especially when dried. It is one of three plants to be called All-heal, the other two being Selfheal and Woundwort. Its specific name *officinalis* shows it was used in medicine. Its generic name may be from the Latin *valere,* to be healthy, or from Valerius the Roman physician. The plant is, like Cat-mint, attractive to cats, who roll on it, and apparently the same holds true for rats, and it is said to have been used by ratcatchers as a bait. A peculiarity of the fruit is that the sepals form a feathery pappus after fertilization and this acts as a parachute to carry the seed on the wind.

Habitat: Damp woods, marshy meadows.
Flowers: June and July, pink, in clusters on three terminal branches of the stem, calyx rolled forming a ridge around the base of a tubular corolla which ends in 3-5 lobes, three stamens.
Stem: Erect, unbranched, hairy below, grooved.
Leaves: Pinnate, lower leaves usually stalked, upper leaves stalkless, leaflets lanceolate in five pairs and a terminal leaflet.
Fruit: Single-seeded achenes.

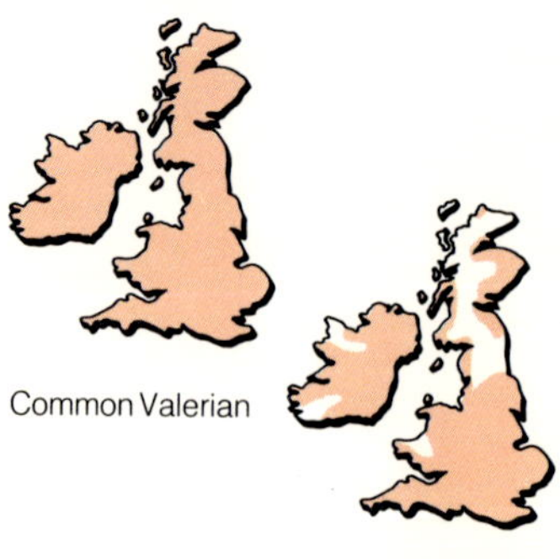
Common Valerian

Common Cornsalad

Common Cornsalad 7-40 cm
Valerianella locusta (2¾-16 in)

Related to the Common Valerian, the Common Cornsalad is a small plant of cultivated ground, an annual with opposite leaves which on the lower part of the stem are slightly spoon-shaped. The stem branches repeatedly into two, with a small group of flowers at the end of each branch. An alternative name is Lamb's Lettuce.

Teasel

TEASEL FAMILY

Dipsacus fullonum 60-200 cm (2-6½ ft)

Dipsacaceae

Other names: Venus's Bath, Venus's Basin

The dried flowerheads of this striking-looking perennial were long used in the manufacture of cloth, for teasing it. Consequently teasel was cultivated, especially around towns and villages where cloth was made. Then a slightly larger kind was imported from the Continent for cultivation. For a long time the two were regarded as separate species, but now the Wild Teasel and the Fuller's Teasel, as they were known, are treated as subspecies of the same species. The flowerheads, which persist through the winter, are today gathered and dyed in different colours and used in floral displays. The other common names derive from another use to which the plant was put. Ladies of fashion used the dew and rainwater collecting in the leaf-bases to bathe their skin to remove freckles and other blemishes.

Habitat: Bare damp ground or ground only sparsely covered with vegetation, riverbanks.
Flowers: July-August, pale purple, in an oval spiny head.
Stem: Erect, stout, sparingly branched, ribbed, prickly, persists with its flowerhead through the winter.
Leaves: Lanceolate, prickly, covered with white pimples, in a basal rosette that withers before the plant flowers, narrower stem leaves clasp stem forming receptacles that catch rain and dew.
Fruit: Small, dry, each containing one seed.

Teasel

Field Scabious

Field Scabious 25-100 cm
Knautia arvensis (10-39 in)

Field Scabious is a beautiful perennial of cornfields and grassy places with mauve and sky-blue flowerheads on long graceful stalks 30 cm (1 ft) or more tall. The basal leaves are lanceolate, the stem leaves deeply indented. The carpels of the flattish flowerheads bear long styles ending in cleft stigmas and look like pins in a cushion.

Harebell

BELLFLOWER FAMILY

Campanula rotundifolia 10-30 cm (4-12 in)

Campanulaceae

Other names: Hairbell, Scotch Bluebell

The Harebell has a delicate beauty which everyone finds irresistible. However, its main claim to fame is the confusion its name gives rise to. First, it is the bluebell of Scotland which is not only totally unrelated to the bluebell familiar to those living in the southern half of Britain but also quite different from it in form. Secondly, why should this dainty perennial apparently be named after an animal? The Rev. C. A. Johns who, in the early years of this century wrote his famous *Flowers of the Field*, was probably more correct in naming it 'hairbell', in allusion to its thread-like stems. The scientific name is also a cause of confusion especially to the beginner. It indicates that it has rounded leaves, but this is true only of the basal leaves. These often disappear at flowering time leaving only the lanceolate leaves.

Habitat: Dry woodland meadows, pastures, heaths, open woodland, on rocks, even on walls.
Flowers: July-October, violet-blue, bell-shaped, on hair-thin stalks, calyx with five sharp points, bell-shaped corolla with five pointed lobes, five stamens, three to five stigmas.
Stem: Very slender, arising from a rootstock.
Leaves: Basal leaves rounded, becoming lanceolate higher up.
Fruit: Capsules still bearing the five-pointed calyx.

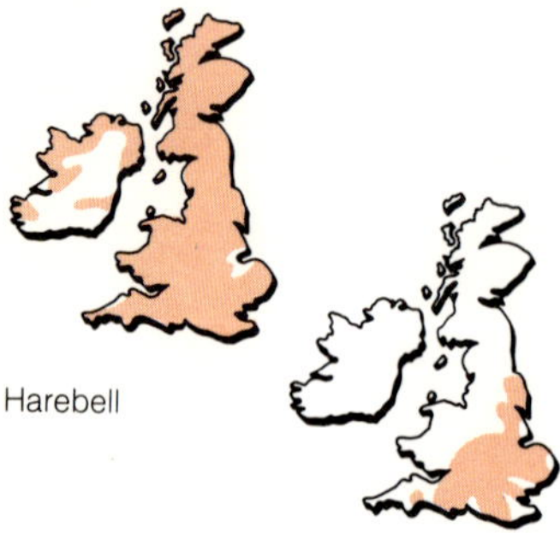

Harebell

Venus's-looking-glass

Venus's-looking-glass 5-30 cm
Legousia hybrida (2-12 in)

Venus's-looking-glass is a very small annual typically found in cornfields and having as alternative names Corn Violet and Corn Bellflower. Up to 30 cm (1 ft) high, its stem and leaves are simple. Its main peculiarity is the unusual length of the calyx tube enclosing the ovary.

Common Ragwort

Senecio jacobaea 60-120 cm (2-4 ft)

DAISY FAMILY
Compositae

Other names: Stinking Willie, Saint James' Wort, Staggerwort, Stammerwort

No one who works the soil for profit or for pleasure is likely to have a good word for the Common Ragwort, a perennial liable to appear almost anywhere. Yet, *en masse*, its golden blossoms undoubtedly add beauty to the landscape. It is the food of the striking yellow-and-black caterpillar of the cinnabar moth and when armies of these have eaten their way through a drift of Ragwort they leave nothing but bare stems with a few tatters of leaves. This could as well be the origin of the plant's name as could the ragged shape of its leaves. The specific name *jacobaea* is after St James, patron saint of horses. Ragwort was once much used in veterinary medicine, and was also used to cure stuttering and stammering, as well as epilepsy. It has an unpleasant smell when bruised.

Habitat: Waysides, waste ground, downland, meadows, almost anywhere on neglected ground.
Flowers: June-October or later, yellow, in compact terminal clusters more or less flat-topped.
Stem: Erect, branching.
Leaves: Pinnate, lyrate, with lobes irregularly toothed giving the leaf a ragged appearance.
Fruit: Achenes with a hairy pappus.

Common Ragwort

Groundsel

Groundsel 8-45 cm (3-18 in)
Senecio vulgaris

A herbaceous annual of disturbed ground which may be found in flower all the year round, Groundsel, like its near relative, Ragwort, bears seeds with a white hairy pappus, so is placed in the genus *Senecio*, from the Latin *senex* meaning 'old'.

Colt's-foot

Tussilago farfara 10-40 cm (4-16 in)

DAISY FAMILY
Compositae

The common name of this perennial is based on the resemblance between the shape of its leaf and that of a colt's hoof. Had Colt's-foot been a native of the Himalayas, some enterprising plant collector might have brought it to Europe where it might have become a treasured garden plant. As things are it remains a beautiful but neglected blossom appearing in late February or March in the most inhospitable of soils. Even so, it was not always so neglected; it was valued as a medicine for coughs and chest complaints generally and, more recently, has been incorporated in herbal tobaccos. When the leaves first unfold they are covered with down, which disappears from the upper surface as the leaf matures. In the days before matches, the down on the undersurface was collected for tinder.

Habitat: Waste or cultivated land especially clay soils.
Flowers: March, yellow, each composite bloom on a single hollow stem covered with large scales, flowers precede leaves.
Stem: Underground rootstock which sends out burrowing offshoots.
Leaves: Broadly heart-shaped, up to 30 cm (1 ft) across, appearing after the flowers have finished.
Fruit: Achenes with a downy pappus.

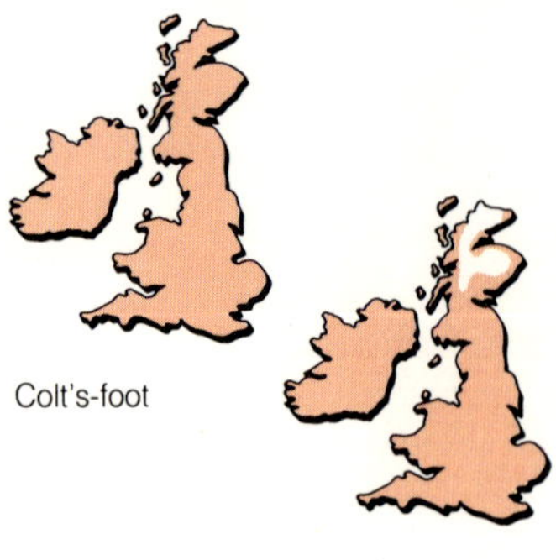

Butterbur up to 150 cm (5 ft)
Petasites hybridus

A perennial growing on the banks of streams or waysides, especially on sandy soils, the Butterbur has much in common with Colt's-foot. It bears its pink flowers in clusters, with male and female flowers mainly on separate plants, and its leaves are up to 90 cm (3 ft) across. It flowers from March to May.

Golden Samphire

Inula crithmoides 10-40 cm (4-16 in)

DAISY FAMILY
Compositae

This perennial is one of the simplest members of the large Daisy family and among the rarest. It is one of three unrelated plants to be given the name 'samphire', the others being the Glasswort and the Rock Samphire, which is a member of the family *Umbelliferae*. All three grow in coastal areas and have fleshy leaves. The name dates from the early 16th century and is said to have started as *perce-pierre*, possibly from Norman-French, on account of the way these plants push their roots into rocks. Then, for no known reason, there was a change to Saint Pierre and then to Samphire. The form of this plant is characteristic of those subjected to an excess of salt. They need to store the fresh water they can obtain and do so in their fleshy stems and leaves.

Habitat: Coastal cliffs, salt marshes, shingle.
Flowers: July-October, orange-yellow, in flat-topped clusters of a few flowers.
Stem: Erect, smooth.
Leaves: Strap-like, fleshy, smooth, sometimes three-toothed at the tips.
Fruit: Hairy seeds.

Golden Samphire

Common Fleabane

Common Fleabane 20-60 cm
Pulicaria dysenterica (8-24 in)

The Common Fleabane is a yellow daisy-like perennial, up to 60 cm (2 ft) tall growing in moist places. Its leaves are large, wavy and hairy. In olden times rushes strewn on the floor provided an ideal breeding ground for fleas, and Fleabane was burnt in the rooms to drive out these insects. The plant was also used as a cure for dysentery.

Common Cudweed

Filago vulgaris 15-20 cm (6-8 in)

DAISY FAMILY
Compositae

Cudweed is an altogether unusual plant, an annual which from the durability of its flowers ranks as an 'everlasting'. Its chief peculiarity, and the character that distinguishes it, is the way the flower stalks are arranged, as described below. This curious mode of growth led the early botanists to dub it *Herba impia*, that is, the undutiful herb, the implication being that the young shoots were guilty of disrespect by overtopping the parents. Why the plant should have been called cudweed is less easy to say. It was so named, it seems, because it was administered to cattle that had lost their cud, though how this was carried out is not clear.

Habitat: Sandy or gravelly places on heaths, waysides and fields.
Flowers: July-August, pale yellow, in clusters of 20-40 rayless flowerheads overtopping the upper leaves.
Stem: Erect, cottony, ending in a globular assemblage of flowers from the base of which are two or more widely divergent flower stalks.
Leaves: Long and narrow, pointed at tip, numerous, overlapping each other spirally up the stem, downy.
Fruit: Seeds with a pappus.

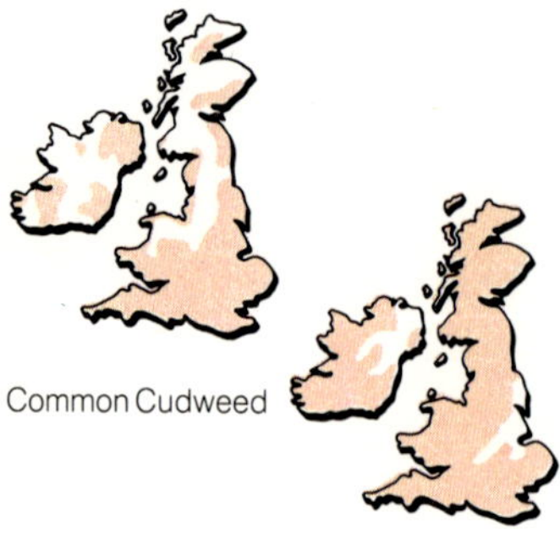

Goldenrod up to 90 cm (3 ft)
Solidago virgaurea

Goldenrod is a tall perennial, up to 90 cm (3 ft) except when growing on cliff-faces when it is only 8 cm (3 in) or so tall. Its leaves are lanceolate with toothed edges. Its golden-yellow flowers are borne on short branches at the top of the main stem, where they form a loose cluster. It was used to treat wounds.

Sea Aster

DAISY FAMILY
Compositae

Aster tripolium 60-90 cm (2-3 ft)

Other names: Starwort, Sea Starwort

Compared with the cultivated asters or the Michaelmas Daisies of the garden, the Sea Aster looks coarse and dingy. It is a stout, succulent perennial which is often seen covered with mud, giving it an unsightly appearance. When it grows on sea cliffs, however, it can be highly ornamental. The flowers consist of a central disc of tiny orange-yellow flowers, outside which is a ring of pale purplish-blue or whitish ray florets, each consisting of a tiny tube with a blue or white strap to one side. The plant has been used as a remedy for eye diseases. We are used to the idea of flowers blooming each in its season. This is determined by the length of day and to some extent by the temperature. Some flowers, like the Sea Aster, bloom only when the days are shortening.

Habitat: Coastal salt marshes, also cliffs.
Flowers: July-September, in clusters at the ends of branches at the top of the main stem, purple-violet, fragrant.
Stem: Erect, slightly branching, ribbed.
Leaves: Oval to lanceolate, long, smooth, fleshy.
Fruit: Seeds with a tuft of white down.

Sea Aster
Daisy

Daisy 2-6 cm (¾-2½ in)
Bellis perennis

The ubiquitous Daisy is the pretty flower that is always with us. It is a perennial and blooms virtually all the year round. It is also the prototype of the family *Compositae*, each flower made up of many florets, some forming a central yellow disc and the ray florets radiating from this. Its name comes from 'day's eye'.

Hemp-agrimony

DAISY FAMILY

Eupatorium cannabinum 30 to 120 cm (1-4 ft) *Compositae*

Hemp-agrimony is a perennial that grows along river banks, in damp woods, fens and damp shaded meadows. It is especially interesting because, although it is included in the family *Compositae*, its flowers do not have the same structure as most members of this family, typified by the Daisy. Each flowerhead looks like a single head but is a collection of five or so tubular flowers surrounded by a calyx of sepal-like bracts. Each of these flowers has a long hairy pappus and the style is very long and deeply cleft into two hairy branches. These serve to sweep the pollen from the anthers so that it is readily available to insects visiting the flowers, which brush against the pollen and carry it to other flowers.

Habitat: Moist shady places.
Flowers: July-October, pink, reddish or nearly white, in flat-topped heads, individual flowers tubular, five or six to a flowerhead, remarkable for deeply cleft styles.
Stem: Rising erect from a woody rootstock, branching at the top, rounded, downy.
Leaves: Broken into three to five lanceolate leaflets, toothed at margins, opposite.
Fruit: Blackish five-angled achenes beautifully plumed with white pappus hairs.

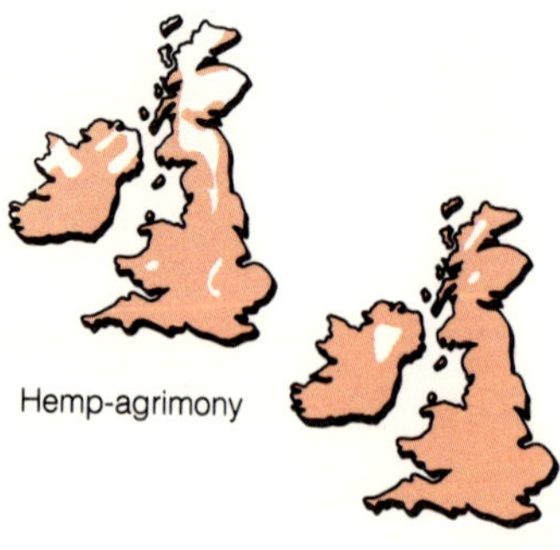

Scentless Mayweed
Tripleurospermum maritimum subsp. *inodorum*
10-60 cm (4-24 in)

The Scentless Mayweed, annual or biennial, looks very like the Corn Chamomile, but whereas this gives out a sweet scent the Mayweed is scentless. It flowers from June to October, its flowers being daisy-like, white with yellow centres. It grows especially on cultivated land.

Yarrow

DAISY FAMILY

Achillea millefolium 30 cm (1 ft) *Compositae*

Other names: Milfoil, Thousand-leaf, Hundred-leaved Grass, Bloodwort, Nosebleed

The large number of common names given to the perennial Yarrow is the surest indication of its popularity. Only a few can be included here. The number is matched by the many medicinal uses to which it has been put. A tea made from it was supposed to banish melancholy. It was used as a most valuable styptic and astringent for wounds and has a reputation as a cure for feverish colds, as a tonic and a blood purifier, and for stimulating the appetite. Botanically it is noted for its deceptive appearance. It looks like a member of the family *Umbelliferae* until its flowerhead is examined closely, when it is seen to have the same structure as a Daisy except that there are usually five ray florets so that each unit of the flowerhead looks like a five-petalled flower.

Habitat: Pastures, waysides, waste land generally.
Flowers: June-November, white, pink or purplish, small, numerous, arranged in a flat-topped mass (corymb).
Stem: Erect, springing from a rootstock, ribbed, slightly tinged with purple.
Leaves: Very finely divided, feathery or fern-like in appearance.
Fruit: Smooth achenes with a rim at the top.

Oxeye Daisy up to 60 cm (2 ft)
Leucanthemum vulgare

The Oxeye Daisy, also called the Moon Daisy, Dog Daisy, or Marguerite, is a perennial growing up to 60 cm (2 ft) tall in pastures, on hedgerow banks and in similar grassy situations. The main stem branches at the top to end in single blossoms and each flowerhead is clothed below with three to four series of scales.

Tansy

Tanacetum vulgare 60-90 cm (2-3 ft)

DAISY FAMILY
Compositae

Other name: Common Tansy

Tansy is an unattractive perennial with a creeping rootstock that is believed to be a garden escape that has become naturalized. If this is so, it is so common that it must be accepted as part of the British flora. It used to be included in every cottage garden and is said to have been a valued item in cookery, in what has been described as 'the nauseous Tansy pudding'. It seems the pudding was served mainly at Easter, as a reminder of the bitter herbs of the Passover. Tansy has a strong scent, especially when bruised. Apparently it was not used medicinally and where the name does appear in herbals it is another name for Yarrow. *Tanacetum* is a contraction of the Greek *athanatos*, meaning immortal or everlasting, and the flowers last a long time after being cut. They are useful therefore in floral decoration.

Habitat: Hedges, waysides, waste ground.
Flowers: July-October, button-like, dull yellow, arranged in a flat-topped cluster, disc florets male only, ray florets short, female.
Stem: Erect, straight, branching above into three or four forks, purplish.
Leaves: Fern-like, alternate, doubly pinnate, each division toothed at edges, lower part clasping the stem.
Fruit: Achenes without pappus.

Tansy

Wormwood

Wormwood 30-90 cm (1-3 ft)
Artemisia absinthium

Wormwood is a common perennial of waste ground. It is a bushy plant with greyish-white leaves and stem, 60 cm (2 ft) high, with numerous small inconspicuous, yellow flowerheads. Aromatic but bitter it was formerly used in brewing beer, before hops were used, and yields the flavouring for absinthe.

Greater Burdock

Arctium lappa 90-200 cm (3-6 ft)

DAISY FAMILY
Compositae

Other name: Common Burdock

The Greater Burdock might almost have been designed specifically for the amusement of small boys who delight in throwing the burrs so that they cling to the clothing of their elders. This alone should be sufficient to identify the plant, except that there is a second, similar species, the Lesser Burdock. The latter has heart-shaped basal leaves, longer than they are broad, whereas the Greater Burdock has rounded leaves as long as they are broad. Also, the smaller species grows no more than 90 cm (3 ft) tall while the Greater Burdock sometimes achieves as much as 2 m (6 ft). Both are biennial. The function of the burrs is to disperse the seeds, and they can be a nuisance sticking to our clothes. They also cling to the wool of sheep and the coats of other mammals.

Habitat: Margins of fields, waysides, waste ground.
Flowers: July-September, with small, pink to purple tubes closely crowded together in a flowerhead and virtually hidden in a ball of green bristles.
Stem: Stout, erect.
Leaves: Basal leaves large, rounded, coarse, wrinkled, with wavy edges, stem-leaves smaller, alternate.
Fruit: Achenes enclosed in scales bearing hooked bristles.

Spear Thistle up to 120 cm (4 ft)
Cirsium vulgare

Spear Thistle, or Spear Plume Thistle, is another pest of farmland. It also is a biennial and it grows to 1.2 m (4 ft) especially in meadows and pastureland. If not cut before flowering it produces a large crop of plumed seeds that are dispersed by the wind. Its stem and leaves are abundantly clothed in prickles that are painful to the touch.

Cornflower

Centaurea cyanus 30-60 cm (1-2 ft)

DAISY FAMILY
Compositae

Other names: Bluebottle, Corn Blue-bottle

The Cornflower is one of the prettiest of our wild flowers. Annual to biennial, it was traditionally associated with poppies and ears of wheat. With modern efficient methods of cleaning the wheat seeds, however, both Cornflowers, in particular, and poppies have become rarer. Cornflower petals were used as a source of a dye for linen and, mixed with cold alum water, for water-colours. The likelihood is that the plant reached Britain from Europe in prehistoric times with early agriculture. It is ironic that since then it has spread widely over the world, with imported grain seeds, and yet is now so rare in Britain.

Habitat: Cornfields especially.
Flowers: May-August, flowerheads at the end of the stem branches, each made up of a cup clothed in green scales above which are two kinds of florets, those in the centre small and purple with an outer ring of blue tubular florets ending in seven tooth-like lobes.
Stem: Erect, slender, sparsely branched.
Leaves: Pinnately lobed, upper leaves strap-shaped, with smooth edges.
Fruit: Achenes with a tuft of reddish hairs.

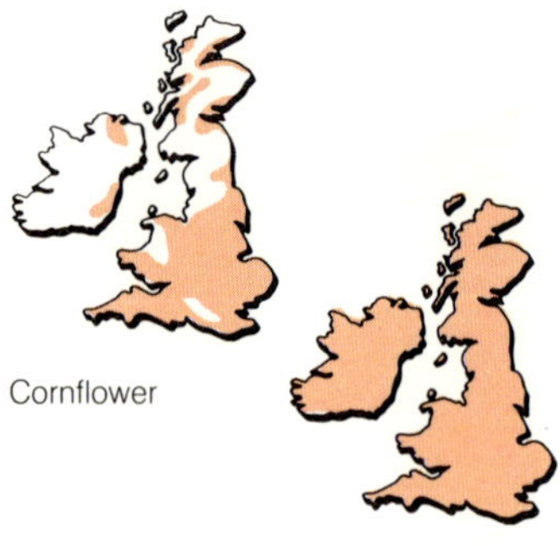

Cornflower

Common Knapweed

Common Knapweed 15-90 cm
Centaurea nigra (6-36 in)

The Common Knapweed is sometimes called the Cornflower and it has to be admitted that the two plants are very similar except that the Knapweed is coarser in every respect. This is reflected in the alternative name of Hardhead. Its flowers are dull purple and it is a perennial, not an annual, like the Cornflower.

Hawkweed

DAISY FAMILY

Hieracium murorum 30-90 cm (1-3 ft)

Compositae

Other names: Few-leaved Hawkweed, Wall Hawkweed

Two explanations have been offered for the name of this plant. One is that the various species of Hawkweed grow in the precipitous places where hawks live; the other, which dates back to Pliny the Roman naturalist, is that hawks feed on the plant to improve their eyesight. *Hieracium* is from the Greek *hierax*, a hawk, but that merely means that the early botanists chose to perpetuate an ancient romantic myth when choosing the scientific name. Botanically, the Hawkweed is closely related to the Dandelion and like it is perennial. The structure of its flowers is basically that of the Dandelion except that there are fewer florets to each blossom. To counterbalance this, a Hawkweed has many more flowerheads. A peculiarity of Hawkweeds is that they tend to reproduce by apomixis; that is, they can form seeds without the fusion of male and female cells.

Habitat: Grassy places, rocks, walls.
Flowers: June-August, yellow, in flowerheads, few in the cluster.
Stem: Erect, hairy, branching.
Leaves: Basal, in rosettes, few, oval to lanceolate, stem leaves few, lanceolate with forwardly directed teeth on margins.
Fruit: Achenes.

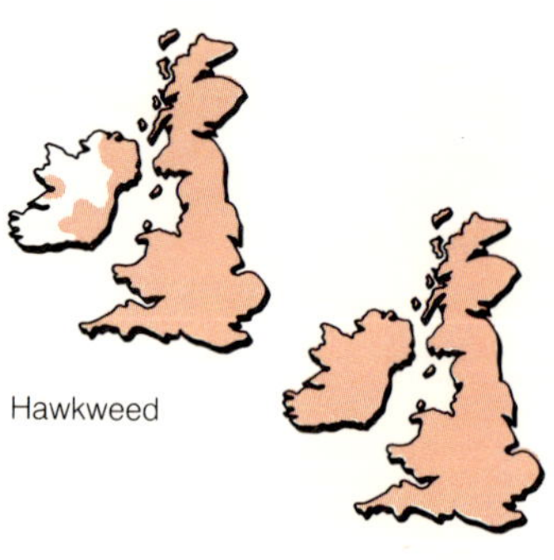

Dandelion 10-30 cm (4-12 in)

Taraxacum officinale

The perennial Dandelion needs no more introduction than the Daisy, both being so ubiquitous and familiar. The Dandelion has long been used as a diuretic which gave rise to the superstition that handling it led to bed wetting. The common name is from the French *dent-de-lion*, from the toothed margins of its leaves.

Water-plantain

WATER-PLANTAIN FAMILY

Alisma plantago-aquatica 30-90 cm (1-3 ft) *Alismataceae*

Other name: Great Water-plantain

It comes as something of a surprise to find that this herbaceous perennial, with its roots in the mud under water, should be more nearly related to the lilies than to the plants so far considered. Despite its name and appearance, the Water-plantain is one of the monocotyledons, whereas all the species described up to this point are dicotyledons. These two groups into which the flowering plants are divided differ markedly. The seeds of dicotyledons have two seed-leaves (or cotyledons). Their leaves are usually net-veined and their flower parts are in fives, fours or multiples of these. The seeds of monocotyledons have only one seed-leaf; their leaves are usually parallel veined and the flower parts are in threes. Thus, the Water-plantain flower has three sepals and three petals. It is regarded by some botanists as a link between these two large groups, the dicotyledons and the monocotyledons.

Habitat: Margins of rivers, lakes and ponds.
Flowers: June-August, lilac, small, delicate, three-petalled on long stalks, in whorls forming a loose pyramidal spray on a tall stem.
Stem: Erect, hairless.
Leaves: Broadly lanceolate, all springing from the roots, strongly ribbed like those of the Plantain.
Fruit: A cluster or whorl of single seeds.

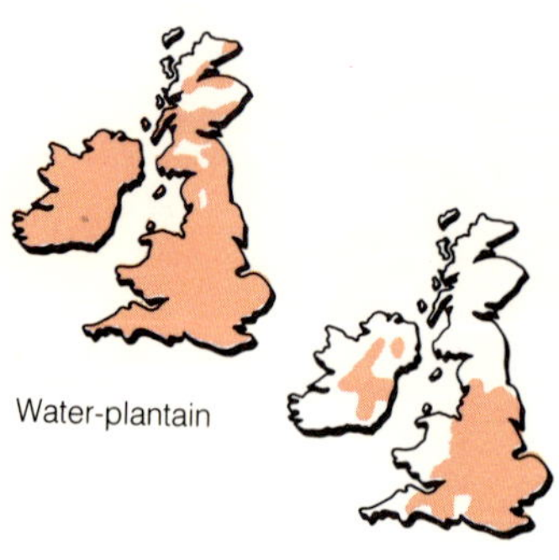

Water-plantain

Arrowhead

Arrowhead 30-90 cm (1-3 ft)
Sagittaria sagittifolia

This is also an aquatic perennial. Its flowers are three-petalled, white with a yellow centre, beside which is a purple spot, and its large leaves are shaped like arrowheads, except in fast streams when the leaves are on the surface and lance-shaped or submerged and ribbon-like.

Broad-leaved Pondweed

Potamogeton natans up to 5 m (16½ ft)

PONDWEED FAMILY
Potamogetonaceae

Other name: Floating Pond-weed

This perennial is one of nine related species all much alike, some living in swampy areas near the shores of ponds, others in deeper water, the species differing mainly in the form of the leaves. The flowers are much reduced. They have only vestiges of sepals and petals, with four stamens and four carpels. After fertilization the carpels form achenes each of which contain air-spaces. These make the seeds buoyant so that they are dispersed and distributed by water. As time goes by the air seeps out of the achene so that it sinks to the bottom of the pond or ditch. There it remains and in due course germinates.

Habitat: Ponds, ditches.
Flowers: May-September, in cylindrical spikes of small, green flowers that rise above the water.
Stem: Long, supple, submerged.
Leaves: Upper (floating) elliptical, stalked, ribbed, leathery; lower (submerged) strap-shaped.
Fruit: Small achenes.

Frogbit 60-90 cm (2-3 ft) long
Hydrocharis morsus-ranae

Frogbit is an aquatic perennial that throws up three-petalled white flowers in July and August. From the family *Hydrocharitaceae*, it produces large buds on its submerged stems in autumn. These fall away and pass the winter dormant on the beds of lakes and ponds. Fresh plants also arise on branches of the main stems.

Solomon's-seal

LILY FAMILY

Polygonatum multiflorum 60-120 cm (2-4 ft)

Liliaceae

This is an unusual perennial that grows from a curiously jointed underground stem. The generic name is based on this stem and is from the Greek *polys*, meaning 'many', and *gonu*, a small joint. From this stem arise leafy stems which grow erect at first and then curve over in an arch from which the numerous leaves and the bell-shaped flowers, in clusters of two to five, hang down. Solomon's-seal (a translation of the medieval Latin *sigillum Solomonis*) is said to be so named because the flowers edged with green look like an old-fashioned seal or because the leaf-scars on the underground stem recall the impression made by a seal, or even because it was good for 'sealing', i.e. knitting broken bones.

Habitat: Woods.
Flowers: May-June, white drooping bells, edged with green, formed from a perianth of six lobes, in clusters of two to eight all turning the same way.
Stem: Drooping, rounded, smooth, springing from an underground stem.
Leaves: Elliptical, alternate, all turning one way, as with the flowers.
Fruit: Red or blackish berries.

Solomon's-seal

Butcher's-broom

Butcher's-broom 60-120 cm (2-4 ft)
Ruscus aculeatus

Butcher's-broom, aptly called at times Knee Holly, is a perennial shrub growing from a stout rootstock and throwing up stems 60-120 cm (2-4 ft) high. Its sharp-pointed heart-shaped 'leaves' are flattened stems or phyllodes; the small white flowers, and later dark-red berries, are borne in the centres of the phyllodes.

Fritillary

LILY FAMILY

Fritillaria meleagris 12-38 cm (5-15 in)

Liliaceae

Other name: Snake's Head

There are certain wild flowers that because of their rarity and beauty make the heart of a botanist leap at sight of them. The perennial Fritillary is one of them. It is very rare, only to be found in eastern and southern England, and even there it is severely localized – it is one of the few of our wild flowers virtually restricted to damp meadows. Its name is from the Latin *fritillus*, a dice-box, supposedly from the shape of its solitary flowers, although it is difficult to see where this resemblance lies. The specific name *meleagris* is from the Greek for speckled. The Fritillary's most famous locality is Magdalen Meadow at Oxford, where it is protected.

Habitat: Damp meadows.
Flowers: April-May, bell-shaped, chequered with dark or reddish-purple squares, with a glistening 'tear-drop' gland at the base inside each segment of the perianth.
Stem: Flower-stalks smooth, erect, springing from a bulb.
Leaves: Blade-like, grooved.
Fruit: Capsules rounded, three-chambered.

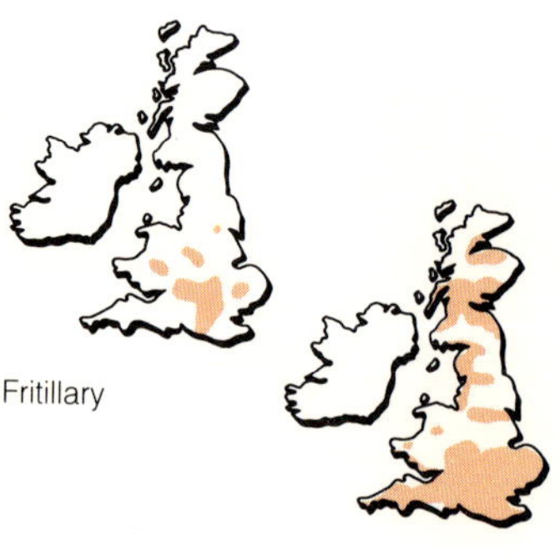

Fritillary

Star-of-Bethlehem

Star-of-Bethlehem
Ornithogalum umbellatum
25-36 cm (10-14 in)

The Star-of-Bethlehem, growing about 30 cm (1 ft) high from a white bulb, has narrow limp leaves and white flowers marked with a broad, central green line on the outside of each segment of the flower. The flowerhead is more or less flat-topped, the flowerstalks being of unequal length. This perennial's flowers open only in sunny weather.

Bluebell

LILY FAMILY

Endymion non-scriptus 20-50 cm (8-20 in)

Liliaceae

Other name: Wild Hyacinth

The Bluebell, not to be confused with the bluebell of Scotland or Harebell (see page 146), is almost too familiar to need detailed description. When left undisturbed, and it is a perennial, it can form huge carpets of blue which delight the eye and proved irresistible to the flower-picker, in the days when wild flowers were unprotected. The specific name *non-scriptus*, meaning 'not written', requires explanation. The name Hyacinthus was given originally to a species of lily with petals marked with dark spots, supposed to form the Greek word *Ai*, meaning 'alas'. The legend was that the youth Hyacinthus had been changed into a flower by Apollo. The Bluebell lacks these spots, and so can be said to be 'without writing'.

Habitat: Open woods, especially where the sun penetrates, among scrub, hedgebanks, seacliffs.
Flowers: April-June, azure blue, occasionally white or pink, in a curved, one-sided cluster of up to 20 bell-shaped flowers with tips of segments out-curved.
Stem: Short and stout, hidden among the storage leaves of the bulb.
Leaves: Long, strap-like, keeled, enlarged slightly at the tip forming a slight hood.
Fruit: Oval capsule with small black seeds.

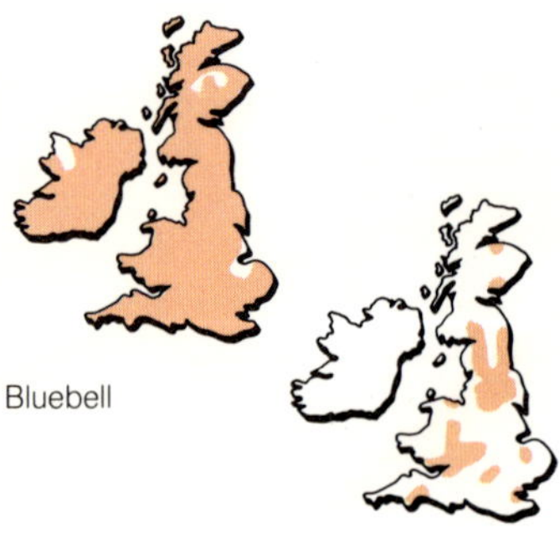

Bluebell

Ramsons

Ramsons 20-25 cm (8-10 in)
Allium ursinum

The most common of the garlics is the Ramsons or Broadleaved Garlic. It is a perennial which grows in woods and on shady banks by means of underground stems from which arise broad, oval leaves pointed at their tips. Each flower stalk bears about 15 star-shaped white flowers with parts in threes or multiples of three.

Field Wood-rush

RUSH FAMILY
Juncaceae

Luzula campestris 10-30 cm (4-12 in)

Other name: Sweep's Brush

The Field Wood-rush is a perennial with a slender rootstock which may well be missed because it looks so like an insignificant kind of grass except when in flower. Even then, it requires close inspection for its delicate beauty to be appreciated. It is one of the first grass-like flowers to bloom in spring and can be distinguished from all other meadow plants by its close cluster of brownish-green flowers marked with the light yellow of its anthers. The Field Wood-rush is a typical monocotyledonous plant with a perianth of six parts, the same number of stamens and an ovary divided into three. It is wind-pollinated and the style bears three greenish-white hairy stigmas that twist together into a spiral after flowering is finished.

Habitat: Meadows, grassy places in woods and on heaths.
Flowers: March-May, chestnut-brown with transparent margins, in clusters on unequal stalks at the head of the stem.
Stem: Erect, slender.
Leaves: Grass-like, margins fringed with weak hairs completely sheathing the base of the stem, with long hairs at the top of the sheath.
Fruit: Triangular capsules, each with three erect seeds.

Field Wood-rush

Wild Daffodil

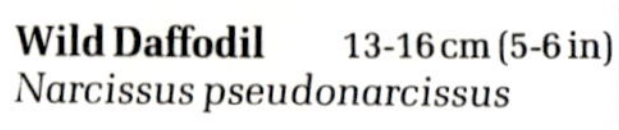

Wild Daffodil 13-16 cm (5-6 in)
Narcissus pseudonarcissus

The Wild Daffodil (family *Amaryllidaceae*) springs from a bulb, and is therefore perennial, from which are thrown up sword-shaped leaves. The flower stalk bears a dry, skin-like spathe which opens to reveal a golden trumpet with a wavy margin surrounded at the base by six pale yellow perianth segments. Also known as Lent Lily.

Yellow Iris

IRIS FAMILY
Iridaceae

Iris pseudacorus 40-150 cm (16-60 in)

Other name: Flag

The Yellow Iris is a stout aquatic perennial growing from a thick rootstock with creeping acrid roots which yields a black dye. It is said that its seeds were roasted and ground and used to make a substitute coffee. However, the plant's main interest is in the peculiar structure of the showy flowers. Their parts are in the threes usual in a family of monocotyledons, but the three sepals are more petal-like than the petals which are small, narrow, erect and curving towards the heart of the flower. The style is broad and arching, and coloured like a petal. This leaves the sepals which form the largest, most striking part of the flower.

Habitat: Watersides, ditches, marshes, swamps.
Flowers: June-July, erect, bright yellow, in twos or threes, springing from a sheathing bract at the top of a stout stem.
Stem: Erect, stout, somewhat flattened.
Leaves: Stiff, erect, sword-shaped with sharp-edged margins, springing from a thick, fibrous, creeping rootstock.
Fruit: Elliptical capsules, pointed at the free end, containing rows of orange-coloured seeds.

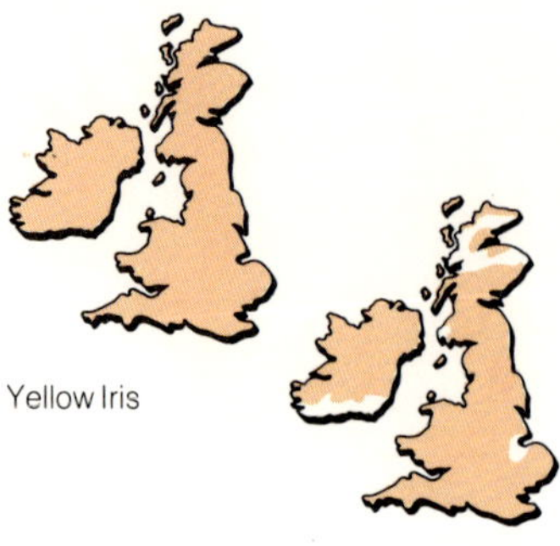

Yellow Iris

Common Twayblade

Common Twayblade 20-60 cm (8-24 in)
Listera ovata

The Common Twayblade (family *Orchidaceae*) bears small green flowers in May and June. If the flowers, carried in a long spike, are inconspicuous the same cannot be said of the plant itself. It grows in woods and pastures up to 60 cm (2 ft) tall from a creeping perennial rootstock. Note the pair of opposite oval leaves halfway up the stem.

Bird's-nest Orchid

Neottia nidus-avis 15-45 cm (18 in)

ORCHID FAMILY
Orchidaceae

The Bird's-nest Orchid is a perennial that lacks chlorophyll. Its stem, leaves and flowers are an unattractive pale brown. It grows in the densest shade, such as in beechwoods, where little sunlight penetrates and is able to do so because it is a saprophyte (i.e. a plant that lives on dead and decaying plant or animal matter), and draws nourishment from the leaf mould under trees. Its common name reflects the tangle of roots which look just like a bird's nest that is made of interwoven twigs. It is the presence in these roots of the threads or hyphae of a fungus that enables it to adopt an unusual life-style. These act as root-hairs, absorbing nourishment which is used by the orchid.

Habitat: Shady woods, especially beechwoods.
Flowers: June-July, pale brown clustered in a dense spike at the end of the stem.
Stem: Erect, fleshy, springing from a mass of roots which are short fleshy fibres.
Leaves: Absent, replaced by brown scales sheathing the stem.
Fruit: Capsules containing numerous small seeds.

Bee Orchid 15-60 cm (6-24 in)
Ophrys apifera

The distinctive character of the Bee Orchid is indicated by its name. A perennial bearing spikes of purple flowers, its individual flowers are pinkish with a three-lobed lower lip that is brownish-purple patterned to resemble the rear end of a bumblebee waiting to enter the bloom. The habitat of the Bee Orchid is grassland and scrub.

Lords-and-ladies

ARUM FAMILY

Arum maculatum 30-50 cm (12-20 in)

Araceae

Other names: Cuckoo Pint, Wake Robin, Jack-in-the-pulpit

The tuberous rootstock of this perennial is nearly 30 cm (1 ft) below the surface of the ground. From this, in March, arise the purple-spotted, arrow-shaped leaves. From the middle of the leaves, in April, emerges a pale-green shoot that develops into an enormous sheath. This opens and unrolls into a hood to reveal a purple column which bears the flowers around its lower part. Above the flowers are hair-shaped structures below which are crowded rings of male flowers, each consisting of a single stamen, and below these are rings of female flowers each no more than a single carpel. Small insects, such as midges, attracted by the foetid odour of the plant, creep past the hairs but cannot get out again until the hairs wither. Meanwhile, they fall down and pollinate the female flowers. Then the male flowers shed their pollen on to them so that when they eventually escape they pollinate the next plant they visit.

Habitat: Woods, copses, waysides, cultivated ground.
Flowers: April-May, arranged on a long fleshy axis enclosed in a large green sheath with a series of male flowers followed lower down by the female flowers.
Stem: Underground, an irregularly shaped tuber.
Leaves: Arrow-shaped, marked with purple spots.
Fruit: Red poisonous berries.

Lords-and-ladies

Common Duckweed

Common Duckweed 4-5 mm (¼ in)
Lemna minor

The Common or Lesser Duckweed (family *Lemnaceae*) is a very small plant that can cover the surface of stagnant water. Each plant consists of a single leaf bearing one root. It has, at times, one or two stamens and one- to four-seeded ovaries on the margin of its single leaf. No sepals or petals.

Glossary

Achene. A small dry seed-like fruit like a tiny nut.
Annual. A plant that lasts only one year or a season.
Anther. That part of the stamen which contains the pollen.
Apical. At the tip or summit.
Axil. The angle between a leaf and a branch or a stem.
Berry. A succulent fruit with seeds immersed in the pulp.
Biennial. A plant flowering in the year following that in which the seed germinates.
Bract. A modified leaf at the base of a flower or flowerstalk; also leaves around a flowerhead.
Bulbil. A small bud.
Calyx. The outermost, usually green, envelope of a flower.
Capsule. A fruit which when dry splits to release the many small seeds it contains.
Carpel. One or more divisions of an ovary or fruit.
Corolla. The collective name for the petals.
Corymb. A flattish topped collection of flowers.
Deciduous. Said of a plant that sheds its leaves.
Dicotyledons. Plants whose seeds have two seed-leaves.
Entire. Said of leaves with margins not toothed or divided.
Floret. One of the little flowers that make up the flowerhead of the *Compositae*.
Follicles. A capsule that opens on one side only.
Fruit. The fertilized and mature ovary or carpel.
Inflorescence. A mass of flowers on a stem.
Lanceolate. Shaped like a lance-head.
Linear. Long, narrow leaf with parallel sides (needle-shaped).
Lobe. A rounded projection, as in ear-lobe.
Lyrate. Shaped like a lyre.
Monocotyledons: Plants whose seeds have one seed-leaf.
Nectary. A group of cells secreting nectar.
Node. Place where a leaf is attached to a stem.
Opposite. Inserted at the same level, as leaves on a shoot.
Ovary. The female part of a flower, represented by the carpels.
Palmate. Somewhat in the form of a hand.
Pappus. A circle or tuft of bristles or hairs, especially used for the modified calyx of the *Compositae*.
Perennial. Lasting more than two years.
Perianth. Outer covering of a flower showing no distinction between sepals and petals.
Petiole. The stalk of a leaf.
Phyllodes. Flattened leaf-stalks or petioles arranged laterally on a stem and functioning as leaves.
Pinnate. Feather- or fern-like leaf-shape in which elongate leaflets form pairs on opposite sides of the leaf-stalk.
Pistil. Seed-bearing organ of a flower, consisting of an ovary, style and stigma.
Procumbent. Trailing on the ground.
Rootstock. An underground stem.
Seed-leaf. Leaf contained in a seed.
Sepal. One of the green leaves forming the outer covering of a bud.
Series. A number of items of one kind arranged in a line, more or less continuously.
Sessile. Sitting directly on a base, without a stalk.
Spathe. A large enveloping leaf or leaf-like structure.
Spike. Terminal stalk covered with unstalked flowers.
Stamen. The male organ of a flower.
Stem leaf. A leaf carried on the stem, as contrasted with one springing direct from the roots.
Stigma. The tip, usually fleshy, of the style.
Stipule. Green leaves, always in pairs, at the base of a leaf or leaf-stalk.
Stolon. Shoot from base of plant.
Style. The slender rod of the pistil running up from the ovary to the stigma.
Subtend. To extend under so as to embrace.
Tap root. A stout, elongated primary root.
Trefoil. A leaf divided into three leaflets.
Trifoliate. Having three leaves growing from the same point.
Tuber. A fleshy underground part of the stem.
Umbel. Arrangement of flowers springing from a common centre and forming a flat or rounded cluster.
Whorl. Arranged in a circle around an axis.

Index Botanical names

Index English names

NB: The plants' alternative names are also listed in this index

PDO 83-1225